How To Respond
At The Crossroad

My Marriage Is In Crisis, Fix It Lord, Fix It!

To Ayana
It has been
a pleasure meeting
you.

P Shope Ansie!

How To Respond
At The Crossroad

My Marriage Is In Crisis, Fix It Lord, Fix It!

Kimberly Bracewell-Thorpe, LMSW

HOW TO RESPOND AT THE CROSSROAD
Published by Purposely Created Publishing Group™
Copyright © 2018 Kimberly Bracewell-Thorpe
All rights reserved.

Printed in the United States of America

ISBN: 978-1-948400-26-8

Special discounts are available on bulk quantity purchases by book clubs, associations and special interest groups. For details email: sales@publishyourgift.com or call (888) 949-6228. For information logon to: www.PublishYourGift.com

Dedication

I dedicate this book to everyone who has loved and lost and to those who continue to evolve and transform for the sake of love. This book is for all the couples that have been at the crossroads in a relationship(s) and those who are currently at a crossroad in their relationship. This book will provide answers for those who are seeking guidance and direction on how to take the road less traveled when they find themselves at a crossroad in a relationship.

The crossroad is a figurative destination at which 40 percent to 50 percent of all relationships plateau. It is at the crossroad that couples are forced to make a decision about the future of their relationship. When a couple reaches the crossroad, two things are clear. 1. Continuing the relationship as it is is not an option, and 2. The couple must decide what the next step is (staying together or separating). Couples arrive at the crossroad for a myriad of reasons. But what happens at the crossroads will impact their future for many generations to come.

This book is geared toward supporting couples in making a healthy decision at the crossroad. This book is not intended to condone or encourage violence. If you are currently experiencing physical or mental abuse in your current relationship (married, dating, engaged), please contact your nearest domestic violence shelter for safety, counsel, and direction. Separate yourself from the abuser ASAP.

I will conclude this dedication by acknowledging my beautiful family. I dedicate this book to all of them as a token of my appreciation for being patient as I stole time away from them to research and write this book. I pray that this book will be a blessing to our family. As I write this book, I am thinking of family, friends, and strangers I have had the privilege of walking with, teaching, and nurturing through crossroad moments. I also have in mind those who read this book whom I will never have the pleasure of meeting, but whom I pray will be blessed by these words. It is my vision that this book will impact marriages in my family and outside of my family for many generations to come. I declare that the information in this book will minister to my seed and my seed's seed. I pray that we will all be inclined to use the tools in this book to bend us toward God and a desire to honor the marriage covenant at all costs.

Table of Contents

Acknowledgments

To my wonderful, patient, God-fearing, anointed, and appointed husband, Eliakim Thorpe, I love you and I am so grateful to God for directing you to choose me over and over again, crossroad after crossroad. Thank you, my dear husband, for loving me through my mistakes, accepting my apologies, guiding me, praying with me and for me, and preparing me for Christ's return. You are beyond awesome. Words can't describe how amazing it has been to love you, allow myself to be vulnerable, and be loved by you. Thank you.

To my beautiful children: Shalibria, Lauren, Kareem, Aniya, and Naomi. I am so grateful that God has given me the opportunity to love and nurture you all. Being in relationship with each of you has grown me in so many different ways. I will continually sacrifice all that I have and all that I am to be in a healthy relationship with each of you.

To my wonderful brother Bobby Bracewell Jr. Thank you for always supporting, encouraging, and loving me.

Thank you for reminding me of our humble beginnings and keeping me grounded so that I am careful not to think too highly of myself. Thank you for always directing me to God when I am in search of answers. God bless our parents, who did the best they knew how to do for us before their very early departure to heaven. I will be forever grateful for the experience of being parented by them and growing up with you and our beloved sister Angela, who also met a very untimely death. I would not trade the experience of being a part of the Bracewell family for anything in this world. That experience made me taller, and I will cherish it forever.

To Yolanda Carr-Johnson, my bestie since 7th grade, an author in her own right. I am still waiting on that book on the inside of you. Thank you for being one of my biggest cheerleaders and making me feel like I can leap tall buildings and take over the world. You have had my back since 7th grade, and I do not take it lightly. This chick will "kill a brick and drown a rock for her bestie." I love you always.

To countless friends who have listened to me talk about marriage and how much I despise divorce, even as some of you journeyed through it (Ebony, Eatonia, Eleanor, Lora, Nita, Regina, Rena, Rockelle, Shana, Sharon, Vanessa, and Yvonne). Thank you for always being my sounding board, my support, and my encouragers. You all have been with me through some tough times, and for that I am grateful. You know who you are. I love and appreciate each of you for being you and allowing me to be me.

Introduction

This book was birthed out of my experience at the crossroad. My crossroad experience is defined as the moment in our marriage when I felt inclined to make a decision about whether or not I should divorce my husband or fight for our marriage. At the height of emotions during the crossroad experience, I recall going to a bookstore looking to find a book that would answer the very question that this book answers: what to do at the crossroad. My hope is that you will read this book and learn how to navigate during your crossroad experiences. I also hope that readers will learn how to avoid crossroad experiences. My intent is to direct readers to God and to learn more about themselves and therefore become more focused on their individual purpose and destiny and less focused on one another's flaws. As you read, take the opportunity to work through and challenge some of your thoughts.

Identify Your Marriage Mentality

How Does Your Mentality Impact Your Marriage?

Let's discuss modern-day mentalities. What are some modern-day mentalities with which you are familiar?

I Win Mentality: It is okay for the husband and wife to compete with each other and not be on one accord concerning matters of the home.

"Do two walk together unless they have agreed to do so?" - Amos 3:3, NIV

Other Woman Mentality: If a man does not feel respected in his home, it is okay for him to get what he needs from other women who make him feel respected and powerful.

"For the lips of an adulteress drip honey and smoother than oil is her speech" - Proverbs 5:3, NASB

The Ruler Mentality: My spouse is to do as I say, not as I do.

"You husbands in the same way, live with *your wives* in an understanding way, as with someone weaker, since she is a woman; and show her honor as a fellow heir of the grace of life, so that your prayers will not be hindered." - 1 Peter 3:7, NASB

Independent Woman Mentality: I am equal to him. I work, I pay bills, I am intelligent, and I should be able to make decisions concerning our household.

"Wives, submit yourselves unto your own husbands, as unto the Lord" - Ephesians 5:22, KJV

Disposable Mentality: If this marriage does not work or if it is too much work, I will just get a divorce.

"What therefore God has joined together, let no man separate." - Mark 10:9, NAS 1977

Neatly Packaged Mentality: As long as the marriage fits the illusion of what I think marriage should look like, we are good. There may be no growth, change, or movement, but it is a beautifully wrapped package.

"I press toward the mark for the prize of the high calling of God in Christ Jesus." - Philippians 3:14, KJV

Retaliatory Mentality: You hurt me, and I hurt you back. An eye for an eye, tooth for a tooth. You cheat, I cheat. You overspend, I overspend. You curse at me, I curse at you. You lie to me, I lie to you.

"Do not take revenge, my dear friends, but leave room for God's wrath, for it is written: 'It is mine to avenge; I will repay,' says the Lord." - Romans 12:19, NIV

Your mentality (how you see marriage and how you see yourself in your marriage) is the primary indicator of how you function in your marriage. Making adjustments in your marital relationship needs to start with asking yourself the question, "What do I think about marriage? What is my mentality as it relates to marriage?" Our mentality about marriage is formulated through our experiences—not just our personal experiences, but also the experiences of others— as well as factors such as our culture, race, education, gender, religion, and spirituality. Ask yourself, "What have I witnessed or experienced that currently impacts the way that I now see my marriage?"

I have been married for 20 years because I changed my mentality about marriage. Initially, the way I saw marriage had us headed toward divorce on our wedding day. When Eliakim asked me to marry him, of course I said yes. For weeks, I thought about whether or not marrying him was the right thing to do. I talked to God about it, but I wasn't quite sure how to hear from him 20 years ago. All I knew was that it felt right, and he was exactly what I prayed and asked God for. I recall asking several godly women, "How do you know if you are marrying the right person?" No one was able to give me the answer I was seeking, but I decided to marry Eliakim after concluding in my mind that if it did not work, I would just get a divorce. The day I married my husband, my mentality as it related to marriage was that my spouse is disposable. I remember thinking, "If this thing is too difficult, I will just call the quits." Until God changed my mentality about marriage, I functioned in my marriage as if my husband was disposable because that was my mentality. Initially, every time we experienced trouble in our marriage, I threatened to pack up the kids and leave. I eventually passed my mentality onto him. When I stopped threatening to leave, he started threatening to leave.

My initial mentality was formulated by what I had experienced in relationships and by what I observed as a youth in the relationships of those around me. My mentality on my wedding day consisted of more than just seeing divorce as an option. My perception of how a couple should function in a marriage was also impacted.

I was the youngest of my parents' three children, but also my mother's confidant. She confided in me about her marital issues. My mother was very passive and soft spoken. My dad was assertive and strong. I observed him dominating my mother in their marital relationship. I despised the way he treated her so much that I recall promising myself that I would never allow a man to ever take advantage of me. When I was older and began to date, that way of thinking caused me to enter into every relationship on the defense.

Now at the opposite end of the spectrum, I had two aunts who were extremely aggressive in their relationships. One of my aunts' husbands cheated on her, and she literally beat him up and divorced him. As a child, I remember secretly cheering for her. My other aunt dated man after man, and I witnessed each of them disappoint her for one reason or another. In retaliation, she did things like cut up their clothing, burn their clothing in the front yard, or slice the interior of their car. When they made her really angry, she would have one of her children put a large pot of water on the stove with sugar in it. The moment it started to boil, she would grab it and throw it on him. The result of that was a man running and howling. I recall seeing more than one of her boyfriends running out of her home screaming and stripping at the same time. In case you did not know, the hot sugar in the water sticks to the body and causes the burn to last for what likely feels like an eternity in that moment.

After witnessing all of that, my mentality about marriage was just warped. Again, I saw men as disposable, and I also concluded that it was acceptable to hurt them if they hurt me in any way. My mentality also included that if I caught him cheating, I would hurt him and her too.

I was saved with that mentality. Once I began to seek God, He stripped me of the old mentality. He gave me a new mentality, a new way of seeing marriage that was in alignment with His word. God is constantly working on our mentality. That process is never-ending. Every time Eliakim and I have a crossroad moment or experience adversity in our marriage, God is always speaking to us about seeing things through His eyes and not our own. Every time we hit a brick wall in our marriage, it is an opportunity for us to seek Him deeper and become more

7

and more like Him. Spending time at God's feet, meditating on His word, and doing His word changes mentalities.

What is your marriage mentality?

_____

_____

_____

Seeking Direction at the Crossroad

Please note that I will often ask you to meditate throughout this book. When I ask you to meditate, what I am asking you to do is find a quiet place. Sit in a chair or lie down and relax as much as possible. Close your eyes. To start, take 10 deep breaths in through your nose and out through your mouth. Feel your body relaxing, focus on the scripture I provided, or just allow your mind to slow down while you count additional breaths that you are taking in and releasing. Meditate each time for a minimum of 15 minutes to a maximum of 45 minutes.

Chapter 1

The Crossroad

The term crossroad is defined by the Webster's dictionary as "a point at which a crucial decision **must** be made that will have far reaching consequences." The crossroad is a place where everything in the relationship comes to a head, and in order to move forward in any direction, a decision about where to go from here must be made. Couples in relationships experience crossroad moments in and outside of a marital union. My primary focus will be on the marital relationship, but you will find that it is applicable to all relationships.

There is a myriad of events that will lead a couple to have a crossroads moment. Just a few include opposing parenting styles; different philosophies about life; conflicting visions, dreams and pursuit of purpose; incompatible religious beliefs; disrespect; adultery; one not feeling appreciated, seen, valued, or heard; conflict over money or family; needs not being met; not allowing one another to be oneself; frequency/infrequency of sexual activity; spiritual promotion; satanic attack on your family; spiritual elevation; and testing of your faith. To simply sum it up, constant discord is the path that leads to the crossroad where a crucial decision about "where do we go from here" **must** be made.

The crossroad is a place of vulnerability—a virtual place where every couple will be challenged, pressed, and crushed on every side. A meeting at the crossroad in every relationship is inevitable. Even Jesus Christ himself had a crossroad experience on the cross. During his crossroad experience, he said, "Father, if You are willing, **remove** this **cup** from me. Nevertheless, not my will, but Yours, be done." Jesus surrendered to the will of the Father at his crossroad experience. We are Christians, but it appears to be very challenging for us to just do what Jesus did. At the crossroad, we can surrender to God and allow His will to be done. Will you surrender to God at the crossroad?

There are many tears shed at the crossroad—tears of agony and tears of joy. The crossroad is designed by God to be a place where an individual is able to be vulnerable, naked, honest, humble, bendable, and open to seeing God and self. The crossroad is not a bad place as many have depicted it to be. It is a place that welcomes repentance, surrendering, submission, growth, and opportunity to become better than you were when you got there. The crossroad is a place of restoration, deliverance, renewal, or defeat—you choose. It is intended to be a place where you shed yourself of pride, vain, glory, and idolatry. It is a place where you exchange ashes for beauty. It is a place where you surrender the old you to God and put on the new you. The problem is that many of us arrive at the crossroad expecting our mate to do all the changing, unaware that we too must change in order to move forward in the right direction.

At the crossroad, you have the option of becoming a kinder, gentler, more loving, more patient, more forgiving, and more committed to "death do us part." At the crossroads, you also have the option of leaving the way that you came, unchanged and unaffected by the Holy Spirit who revealed Himself to you there at the crossroad. He is there, ready and available to soften your heart, sup with you, comfort you, and deliver you from all that you carried to the crossroad. When we get to the crossroad broken, heavy, confused, afraid, anxious, unsure, and carrying a load too heavy for us to continue to bear as individuals and as a couple, it is the Holy Spirit who awaits, ready to release us of the heavy load and deliver us from the hurt, the pain, the confusion, the uncertainty, and the attack on our marriage/our ministry.

What will you do at the crossroad? Where will you decide to go from here? Before you answer, you must understand that the decision you make at the crossroad does not only impact you, your lifestyle, and the life of your mate. What happens at the crossroad will impact every person who is connected to you and your mate now and into eternity. What you decide at your crossroad moment will determine how those who are connected to you will be impacted.

God speaks of the crossroad in Jeremiah 6:16. He says, "Stand at the crossroads and look; ask for the ancient paths, ask where the good way is, and walk in it, and you will find rest for your souls. But you said, 'We will not walk in it'" (NIV). God was speaking to the sinful people of Jerusalem. He was warning and encouraging them to stand in the midst of everything that was going on around them, ask questions, seek counsel to do what was right, and then walk in it. During our crossroad moments, God is also encouraging us to stand, observe, seek counsel, take the good direction, and walk in it. Just as the people said no to God in scripture, 40 to 50 percent of our population is saying they will not walk in it, and a decision to get a divorce is made at the crossroad. If you will allow me to be transparent, my husband and I came very close to being included in that statistic, and so have so many others. Instead of fighting each other at the crossroad, fight to become victorious over the crossroad experience.

Crossroad Experience:

James and Rachel were high school sweethearts. After dating for a few years, Rachel and James were with child. They became parents at the age of 20. They had a beautiful baby girl. At the age of 21, they both confessed Jesus Christ as their Lord, and they made a decision to get married. They were married at the age of 22. For the first eight years, things were beautiful. Sure, they had their ups and downs, but nothing challenging. There was harmony in the home. They were on one accord with making decisions in the best interest of the family. They attended church together regularly. They both felt a deep connection to the Lord and began to seek Him for their purpose in ministry.

In the ninth year of marriage, James began to feel a "tugging on his heart," as he described it. James informed Rachel that the tugging on his heart was God speaking to him about his purpose. As James increased his time alone with God, God revealed to him that he was chosen to preach the gospel. James and Rachel were very excited about the revelation James received.

In their tenth year of marriage, James began to spend more time with God and less time with Rachel and their daughter. Rachel found herself resenting God. Rachel started to feel rejected and abandoned by James. She saw him changing. He was no longer the man she fell in love with and married.

James' change, although positive, was still difficult for Rachel to adjust to because she felt shut out. Rachel wanted the old James back—the James who always wanted to be with her, cuddle with her, and succumb to her often spontaneous, romantic getaways and impromptu walks and picnics in the park. James was kind about it, but he wasn't able to accommodate Rachel like he had in the past. James was more focused now. His commitment to the word and assisting his pastor with serving the congregation was now his priority. James was excited to serve and to walk in the calling that God had put on his life. Rachel began to feel invisible, unappreciated, and unimportant to James. Rachel attempted to express her feeling to James, but he would often brush her off and explain away his actions by using the scripture. Rachel found herself lashing out at James about small things. Rachel felt alienated and mad all the time. Rachel began to lash out at her co-workers and her daughter. Rachel did not like the person she had become.

James felt like Rachel did not support him, his purpose, or the plan that God had for their family. James also felt disrespected by Rachel because she had become extremely oppositional. Every interaction between the two of them was contentious.

They had now been married for 13 years, and they were at the crossroad contemplating where to go from here. Neither of them was willing to continue in the union with things the way they were. They both knew that a crucial decision had to be made. Rachel wanted James to see her, spend time with her, and invite her to be a part of what God was doing in his life. James wanted Rachel to respect him, support him, and be patient with him as he pursued his purpose and God-given vision for the family.

<u>Crossroad Experience:</u>

Joseph and Felicia were married when they were in their 30s. This is both of their second marriages. They have a blended family. Joseph has two daughters from his previous marriage and Felecia has two sons from her previous marriage. Together, Joseph and Felicia have one son. Things were going well until Joseph started working late hours and Felicia was no longer in the mood to be intimate late at night when Joseph came home or early in the morning before Joseph went to work. Lack of intimacy made Joseph grumpy and impatient with Felicia and the children. Lack of intimacy and quality time and loneliness made Felicia resent being married for the second time. Felicia wanted more quality time with her husband, and Joseph wanted to have sex with his wife and be appreciated for working long hours to provide for their blended family.

These are just a couple of scenarios that lead couples to a crossroad in their marriage. Although there may be similarities among couples, every couple has their own experience that will inevitably bring them to a crossroad. It is my opinion that every couple will have a crossroad experience. According the American Psychological Association, 40 to 50 percent of all first-time marriages in the United States end in divorce, and 70 percent of second marriages end in divorce. The decision to stay together or get a divorce is made at the crossroad.

Crossroad experiences can be traced back to biblical days. In the book of Esther, King Ahasuerus and Queen Vashti had a crossroad experience. In celebration of his position and military plan, the king held a seven-day drinking feast for men only. According to the Bible, he was drunk. In his drunken state, he ordered his wife to come to the drinking feast, but Queen Vashti refused. It is written in commentaries that she declined to attend because it was not customary for a woman to be at an all-male drinking feast. It is also noted that the king had plans to make a lewd display of her. Like many of us, Queen Vashti knew her husband. And I am going to go out on the limb and say that she was a bit oppositional, and she had good reason to be. The queen did not trust what could potentially happen at the feast. She did not trust the king to cover her in that environment, and she opposed being made a spectacle of. I do not believe that the queen's oppositional behavior was an isolated incident. It is clear to me that she may have been an oppositional queen, and for this reason, the king's court wanted to get rid of her. Being oppositional over time will erode a marital union and turn your mate's heart away from you. Unfortunately, this would be the last time the queen would have an opportunity as the king's wife to refuse to obey him. I imagine that the king and the queen were already at the crossroad when she refused to obey his order in front of his chamberlains, princes, and guests. The queen's disrespectful response to the king's order and his pride and arrogance positioned the king to make a decision. At the crossroad, a decision was made by the king to end the marriage. King Ahasuerus divorced Queen Vashti. At the crossroad, Queen Vashti made a decision not to allow the king to disrespect her and therefore declined his order.

From the looks of it, this marriage was in trouble before the feast occurred. During this crossroad experience, the king accepted counsel from his friends instead of God. This was the error that led so quickly to divorce. When a couple is at a crossroad, it is vitally important that they seek God for direction. It is fine to share and seek the godly counsel of friends and marital advisors, but direction as it relates to where we go from the crossroad should come directly from God.

Assessment:

---

1. What characteristics have I been exhibiting that I need to leave at the crossroad? (Lord, please help me to see me.)

---

2. Where do you think you and your mate should go from
   here? Use scripture to support what you are thinking.
   (As Christians, we have a responsibility to keep our
   thoughts in alignment with God's word.)

_____

_____

_____

3. Do you believe that God put the two of you together
   for a specific purpose? If so, how are the two of you
   supposed to impact the kingdom of God?

_____

_____

_____

4. What kind of legacy does God want the two of you to
   leave?

_____

_____

_____

5. What is your biblical responsibility as it relates to this marriage? (Use Ephesians 5 if you would like to.)

_____

_____

_____

Prayer

God, we are experiencing a crossroad moment. Please help us to deny ourselves and acknowledge You with our whole heart. Lord, not my will nor my mate's will be done, but Your will be done. I stand in agreement with Your word that says, "No weapon formed against us shall prosper, and every lying tongue that rises up against us shall be condemned." Lord, You said this is our heritage. Lord, soften our hearts toward You and each other so that we will become bendable in the direction You will have us go in. Order our steps according to Your word. In the name of Jesus, I command pride, disrespect, selfishness, envy, and jealousy to flee from in and around our union. Lord, bless us to yearn more for each other than the approval of others. Show us how to be a light for You in this dark world, Lord. I cancel out the enemies who plan to bring separation or division into our home. Lord, bless Your Holy Spirit to fill our home with Your love, forgiveness, peace, and harmony. In Jesus' name, I pray. Amen.

Chapter 2
What Should I Do at the Crossroad?

The first thing you want to do at the crossroad is seek God. Set aside time daily to go into your closet (place of prayer). Make a commitment to yourself and God to meet with Him daily in the same place. Make sure this place is private. This should be a place where no one else can hear you but God. Take a journal and a pen into your prayer closet with you. When you go in, just begin to speak to God about where you and your mate are in this relationship. Share with God the present circumstances as you see them. Submit yourself to His will and ask Him to fix it.

Example:

God, my mate and I are at a crossroad.

1. These are the circumstances that brought us here:

_____

_____

_____

2. God, I own and I repent for (my part in the circumstances). I am responsible for:

_____

_____

_____

God, show me what I am missing and direct me into reconciliation with my mate.

Pray this prayer:

> God, I come humbly submitting myself before You knowing that You are Lord and that You can do all things but fail. I am grateful that You are a God who knows my griefs and my sorrows (Isaiah 53:4). God, my mate and I are in trouble in our marriage. God, I am before You today because I want You to fix it, Lord. I want You to help me. Lord, show me how to be the mate You created me to be. Lord, forgive me for:

_____

_____

_____

....

Prayer

God, walk with me and give me direction on where
You would like for me to go from here. God, I need
you right now so desperately to fix this marriage.
God, please make it better than it ever was before.
God, marriage is Your plan. I believe that this is the
mate whom You gave me. God, I want to keep the
covenant I have made with You and my mate. God,
You said that You would not allow any weapon that is
formed against us to prosper. I declare that this crossroad experience will not end in divorce. Lord, I will
trust You in this and through this with all of my heart.
I will not lean to my own understanding of it. I will
acknowledge You in all of my ways, and I know that
You will direct my path. I need You, Lord, to strength-
en me and comfort me through this journey. God, I
know that You are for us. I thank You for being my
God. I thank You for comforting me. I thank You for
never leaving me or forsaking me. I thank You for
Your deliverance power. I thank You for Your healing
and restoration power. Lord, please heal me and my
mate of all of the hurt and the pain that got us to this
crossroad and restore our marriage like only You can.

God, please speak to me throughout this day that I may hear You and be directed in reconciliation with my mate. In Jesus' name, I pray. Amen.

At the crossroad, every couple's faith in God will be tested. Internally, you will need to answer questions like:

1. Is God really who I believe Him to be?
2. Is He really the potter?
3. Can God do His will with unwilling vessels?
4. Does God still do miracles?
5. Can He restore everything that we have lost?

The answer is yes to all five questions. There is nothing that is too difficult for God. I know because my husband and I have also had our crossroad experiences. God has answered yes to all five of those questions for us. If you ask Him, He is responsible for directing you through your crossroad experiences and restoring your marriage.

When we were at the crossroad, I often asked God, "Why?" He repeatedly responded with Isaiah 43:1b-2: "You are mine. When you passest through the waters, I will be with thee; and through the rivers, they shall not overflow thee; when though walkest through the fire, thou shalt not be burned; neither shall the flame kindle upon thee."

I was under the impression that my marriage would not and should not be tested. But God reminded me through Isaiah 43 that He never said that we would not experience trials. What He has made very clear in Isaiah 43 was that we would experience some very uncomfortable situations. In those times, we would feel overwhelmed and even defeated, but He promised to not allow what we are experiencing at the crossroad to overtake us. Even when things got really heated, He promised not to allow the heat of the crossroad experience to consume us. Most important of all in Isaiah 43, He promised that He would be with us.

During your crossroad experience, call on Him. During our crossroad experience, I read many scriptures, but I held close to one in particular. I recited it every time I became angry. I recited it every time I wanted to say something to my husband that was unkind. I recited it instead of responding to things my husband said intentionally and unintentionally to trigger my flesh. I recited this scripture every time the enemy attempted to feed me negative thoughts about my husband and our future. The scripture I held on to dearly is Proverbs 3:5-8 "Trust in the LORD with all thine heart; and lean not unto thine own understanding. In all thy ways acknowledge him, and he shall direct thy paths. Be not wise in thine own eyes: fear the LORD, and depart from evil. It shall be health for thy navel, and marrow to thy bones" (KJV).

Please ask God for a scripture to recite during your crossroad experience. You must hold onto it and rely heavily on the Lord. You are vulnerable to confusion, influence, and coercion at the crossroad. It is at the crossroad that a decision to stay together, separate, or divorce is made. At the crossroad, the enemy will come at you with every tactic that he has to justify separation or divorce. You must be on guard at the crossroad to bring every thought into the obedience of Christ.

At the crossroad, I encourage you to put down your physical weapons. The battle at the crossroad is spiritual in nature. Your physical weapons are no match for the battle at the crossroad, so gird up. Put on the breastplate of righteousness and hold on tightly to the sword of truth. Keep your mind clear so that you can hear the Lord speaking to you at the crossroad. He will give you direction, but if you allow other voices to become louder than His, the direction He desires to send you in will become unclear.

Be patient at the crossroad; don't expect to leave the crossroad as soon as you get there. Be patient and open to learning about yourself at the crossroad. If you allow God to, He will show you who you are at the crossroad and how to become more like Him. At the crossroad, I learned that I was very abrasive toward my husband. I learned that I often disrespected him (knowingly and unknowingly) and that I had been unkind to him over the years. I was not consciously aware of my behavior before our crossroad experience, and it was God, not my husband, who showed me who I had become and how to make the adjustments that would result in me becoming a healthier person. I was clearly under the impression that I had been a great wife and my husband was the luckiest man in the world to have me. Oh yeah, did I mention that God also showed me that I was a bit proud and arrogant? At the crossroad, I learned that I had ignored so many of my husband's needs. The poor man was emaciated from lack of affection, care, and attention. At the crossroad, God also showed my husband who he was and what I needed from him.

Be still. Although you may be uncomfortable and in pain, don't rush through the crossroad experience. I encourage you to use the time at the crossroad to seek God with all of your heart. Be intentional about listening to God more than or as much as you speak to Him. He will reveal everything you need to know in order for you to move forward with clarity. Be careful not to talk to too many people while you are at the crossroad. The list of those you choose to confide in should be very short and directed by God. It is okay to seek godly counsel, but make sure it is godly counsel. You still have the responsibility of covering your mate. Therefore, you should limit your list to only one or two people who share in your commitment to cover your mate and not share your business with others.

List reasons why you should stay in this covenant relationship between you, your mate, and God. (If you are able, please use scripture to support the reasons you should stay in this covenant relationship.)

1. _____

2. _____

3. _____

4. _____

5. _____

6. _____

7. _____

8. _____

List reasons why you should dissolve the covenant relationship between you, your mate, and God. (If you are able, please use scripture to support the reasons you feel you should dissolve this covenant relationship.)

1. _____

2. _____

3. _____

4. _____

5. _____

6. _____

7. _____

8. _____

At the crossroad, it is important for you to be able to see in front of you what you are thinking and asking God to fix. Pray specific prayers using the information above.

Chapter 3
How Do I Put a Stop to the Arguing?

I tried for years on my own to put a stop to the arguing with my mate. But I had a very difficult time bridling my tongue, and over the years, it cost me. I remember feeling like it was going to just kill me if I could not just say one more sharp, sarcastic thing. Year after year, that one more sharp, sarcastic thing slowly ate away at our marriage over and over again. That one more thing that I just could not help but say led us closer and closer to the crossroad. God showed me Ephesians 4:29-32:

> [29] Let no corrupt communication proceed out of your mouth, but that which is good to the use of edifying, that it may minister grace unto the hearers.

> [30] And grieve not the holy Spirit of God, whereby ye are sealed unto the day of redemption.

[31] Let all bitterness, and wrath, and anger, and clamour, and evil speaking, be put away from you, with all malice:

[32] And be ye kind one to another, tenderhearted, forgiving one another, even as God for Christ's sake hath forgiven you. (KJV)

I meditated on this scripture for years, and still I continued to argue. It was not until I went to God and I totally surrendered my tongue to Him that I stopped using my tongue to tear away at our marriage. In exchange for my sharp words, He gave me a scripture on which to meditate. Instead of saying what my flesh wanted me to say, I began to simply recite scripture. I literally recited scripture aloud or in my head each time I wanted to cut into my mate. Total surrender to God and reciting the scripture instead of cutting my mate down with sharp words really worked for us, and the arguing ceased in our home. This is not to say that I was the cause of all of the arguments, but the fact is that in order for an argument to really happen, it takes two people. When I stopped arguing, he had no choice but to stop arguing.

At the foundation of every argument is the inability to keep your thoughts and emotions from coming out of your mouth. Mastering the tongue is key when it comes to avoiding arguments. The Book of Proverbs is quite raw on the subject. Proverbs 29:11 states, "Fools vent their anger, but the wise quietly hold it back" (NLT). You are not a fool. If you have a need to express your anger and just get the words out, write a letter to your mate. In the letter, say everything you are feeling and thinking. Please don't hold back. When you are done and you have gotten it all out, tear the letter up and burn it. It will feel good to have expressed everything you were feeling while avoiding hurting your mate. Another option is to write a letter to God in your journal and tell Him all about what you are feeling and why you are so upset and then ask Him to fix it.

At the foundation of every argument is selfishness. Both parties are fighting for what they believe to be correct and for what they want, even if it is simply just to be correct. Both minds are closed to hearing and understanding what their mate is attempting to express. Before an argument ensues, take some time to step back from pushing your own views or agenda and just listen to your mate. Listen to understand your mate's point of view. Listen for points to agree with your mate about. Listen with intent to show compassion and understanding in areas of disagreement. Arguments are fueled when you are listening just for a chance to speak and defend your position. Instead of a rebuttal, try to understand why your mate feels the way he or she feels. Consider allowing your mate to have whatever he or she is so passionate about, even if it will cost you in a small or large way. Trust God with the situation. Many times, I have listened to my mate introduce what I thought was a ridiculous idea, and instead of fighting or arguing, I just said okay. Then I left his presence

33

and immediately went into prayer, giving the situation, my mate, and the possible outcome over to God. After many arguments, I have learned to abstain from trying to persuade my husband to think like me. I simply state my position. Then I take my concerns to the one who is really in control. The results have varied:

- God has allowed my husband to learn from some mistakes along the way.

- When my husband found no resistance with me, he has concluded to move in a direction I am in favor of.

- God has shown me that my mate is correct and that many of his ideas I opposed have blessed our family.

I learned that my selfish way of seeing and interpreting things is not always correct. I also learned that I can trust God to fix things if my mate messes them up. Coming to this conclusion has been a very humbling experience, and it has taken the pressure off of me to attempt to control my mate, the decisions he makes, and the outcome. Instead, I just trust God.

Refuse to be oppositional. There are so many things to fight about in a marriage: our position, our pride, respect, dignity, money, children, family, extramarital relation-ships, religion—and the list goes on and on. Be clear about this one thing: fighting is useless and counterproductive.

When a couple fights, there is no winner. Fighting only separates you more. Fighting with your mate is not going to make your mate love you more. It will not make your mate desire to be closer to you. It will not make your mate want to spend more time with you or do romantic things for you. Whether you prove yourself to be right or wrong, your mate will not want to be anywhere near you. If you want your mate to desire you, stop arguing, questioning, nagging, and harassing your mate. Arguing creates a negative environment. No one wants to consistently be in a negative environment. Negative energy is a like a repellant.

Arguments usually consist of one partner criticizing the other partner. Criticism from an employer or even a stranger is painful. It is much more painful when it comes from the person who has vowed to love you, support you, be your number-one fan, and cover you. When a person consistently receives criticism from a mate, something on the inside of him/her begins to die. That person will begin to slowly retreat as not to allow themselves to be hurt again. Getting what you want in an argument at the expense of your mate retreating is a heavy price to pay.

If you are for this marriage, recreate the positive environment that the two of you once shared. Recall when your interactions with your mate were positive. Positive energy is magnetic. It draws your mate to you and reminds him/her why he or she fell in love with you in the beginning. Remember how special and important you made your mate feel. Recall how you always greeted your mate with a smile. The energy around the two of you was positive because you made it that way. Recreate that environment. Sure, things have changed over time. What has not changed is your mate's need to be encouraged, to be smiled at, to hear a funny joke, and to share great memories.

Over time, couples begin to take each other for granted, and it is as if they forgot why they chose each other. My bestie has been my best girlfriend since seventh grade because of the way that she makes me feel when I am around her. I chose her as my best friend because she makes laugh, she encourages me, she supports me, and she makes me feel like she needs me and that I am important in her life. I have met many people over the years, but my friends are those who make me feel special and important. I managed to escape having close, meaningful relationships with other women who did not work with me to create a positive environment for our friendship to grow in. A good feeling and positive energy are the foundations for all healthy relationships. A great majority of us surround ourselves with people who make us feel good when we are around them. We walk away from people who do not make us feel good.

What brings many of us to a crossroad experience is no longer wanting to be around the person to whom we have committed our life because there is contention and negative energy in the midst of most of our interactions.

It is imperative that couples be intentional about creating a positive environment for the union to grow and be nourished in. Plan to make your mate laugh more often. Regardless of the circumstances, greet each other with a smile and set aside time to simply recall what the two of you are thankful for. Instead of focusing on what your mate has done wrong, shift to praising your mate for what he or she has done correctly. No one wants to be criticized or condemned for what they do wrong. We would all prefer to be commended for what we do right.

Positive energy is magnetic. It was your positive energy that attracted your mate to you. No one in their right mind goes on a first date exuding negative energy—not if they want a second date. Regardless of what is going on in their life, they pull themselves together and are positive on that first date—and the second and third ones too. If this can be done to please a stranger, certainly we can do it for our mate. One commitment I make to my marriage is not to ever allow a negative environment that makes my mate feel unwelcomed or as if he would prefer to be in alternate environment that is more positive permeate in our home. If your mate chooses to go elsewhere, that is not your fault. Your only responsibility is to do what you can to make your home a positive, welcoming environment. There is no room for arguments in a positive environment. Sure, there will be disagreements that lead to a discussion between two mature adults interested in a solution. Again, that discussion should start with a focus on the things the two of you agree about and end with what is best for the marriage moving forward.

It is very difficult to verbally attack your mate regardless of his or her behavior if you can acknowledge that the real enemy is Satan working through your mate. Imagine this: your mate is under attack by the enemy, and then you jump in and attack your mate too. In reality, you are helping Satan beat down your mate. Your mate acting out of character is a sign that your mate is under attack. Many times, our first response is to attack our mate. Our response should be to get in position and fight the enemy on behalf of our mate. When you do anything other than that, you are falling into the plan of the enemy. Scripture says, "The thief cometh not but for to steal, and to kill, and to destroy" (John 10:10 KJV). Will you allow the enemy to destroy your union, or will you fight back with spiritual weapons? Scripture says, "For the weapons of our warfare *are* not carnal but mighty through God to the pulling down of strong holds" (II Cor 10:4-5, KJV). Recognize who the enemy is and fight with your spiritual weapons for the release of your mate from the grip of Satan. Do not fall for the trick of fighting against your mate with carnal weapons (arguing, criticizing, disconnecting). Use your spiritual weapons (scripture, prayer, fasting, faith, praise). Don't give the enemy any choice but to release your mate. There is no time for arguing. You must immediately go into spiritual warfare with the real enemy. Remember that

God has promised not to leave you or forsake you. He is in the fight on your behalf.

Have you ever found yourself fighting and arguing with people who constantly compliment you or give you praise for everything that you do (big and small)? No, of course not. If you want to create an argument-free environment, be intentional about complimenting your mate. Examples include "Honey, you look nice today," "Good job on the assignment at work," "You are a great parent," "You smell great," "Your skin looks good," "You are beautiful," "You are smart," and "I am blessed to have you as a mate." A pleasant environment disarms strife. According to Proverbs 15:1-2, "1. A soft answer turneth away wrath: but grievous words stir up anger. 2 The tongue of the wise useth knowledge aright: but the mouth of fools poureth out foolishness" (KJV). Again, you are not a fool, therefore keep strife out of your home.

At the core of every human being is the need to feel wanted and important. Instead of arguing with your mate, set aside time daily to make your mate feel wanted by you. If you have been married for several years like me, you may be thinking, "How do I do that?" The answer: the same way you did it when you first met your mate. When I first met my mate, I was so considerate of his needs. I looked for ways to serve him. I surprised him with small tokens that expressed my appreciation of his love. I smiled at him all the time. I always touched him—not in a sexual way, just a soft touch of reassurance.

I initiated going special places with him. I always kissed him. It wasn't until we reached a crossroad in our marriage that I realized I had stopped doing a lot of those things, and as a result, my mate felt unwanted. He felt like I no longer desired him. I did, but I was just busy with running businesses, studying scripture, spending time with friends, and raising five children alongside him. At the crossroad, I realized my error. I repented, I humbled myself, and I made time for my mate again. I went back to doing what attracted him to me and some extra stuff that I was sure would make him feel wanted. My change in behavior disarmed the attack that was coming from his direction, and he immediately began to smile at me again. Presently, between writing this book, attending to our five children, spending time with friends, and running businesses, I am intentional about stopping everything daily just to love up on him and reassure him that I want him. As a result, our home is an argument-free zone. We do still have disagreements, but we are committed to not allowing our differences in opinion or our way of seeing things jeopardize our relationship and spark arguments.

Although I encourage couples to avoid arguing, please note that if there is something to fight about, there is something to fight for. When I was in college, I worked as a patient advocate at a hospital. I had the opportunity to work and support patients and their families during health crises. During the time I worked at the hospital, I enjoyed visiting the babies on the pediatric unit, merely because I love children and the babies often put a smile on my face. One thing that broke my heart on that unit was seeing babies who did not cry. You would think that was a good thing, but I learned that some of the babies were so sick that they stopped crying. It was one of the saddest things I had ever witnessed. It was if the baby had given up. I imagined that the baby was thinking, "I just don't have the energy to cry." The baby just lay in the crib with IVs and tubes coming out of its small frame with no fight left in it. Man, did I pray over those babies, asking God to let His presence be known. I prayed that the babies would feel well enough to cry, to fight, and to pull at the tubes or something. It was amazing to watch the babies' bodies heal. The light came back in their eyes, and they began to cry and pull at the IVs and tubes. It was then that I knew that the baby was on the road to recovery.

Fighting for the relationship is important. It is a sign of life in the relationship. When one partner or the other becomes totally mute and unresponsive in the relationship, refusing to fight for the relationship, it is a sign that the marriage is really in trouble. Fighting against one another is futile, but it is imperative that one or both of you are willing to fight for the relationship. Don't become limp in the marriage and give up. Fight. If you must fight, fight to stay together. Fight to make it work. Fight to humble yourself. Fight to please your mate. Fight to deny yourself. Your willingness to fight is a sign that the relationship is not hopeless.

1. What can I do today to make my mate feel wanted by me?

_____

_____

_____

2. How can I change the environment in our home?

_____

_____

_____

3. What can I do for my mate that will remind my mate of when we first met?

_____

_____

_____

4. **What will I say to build my mate up? How often will I intentionally say nice, encouraging things to my mate?**

_____

_____

_____

5. **Play one of the songs that was sung on your wedding day and remember how you felt on that day. Share the memory and the feeling you felt that day here and again with your mate.**

_____

_____

_____

Give your mate eye contact today and reassure your mate of the fact that you love him/her.

6. **Commit to using your tongue to build up your mate. Write down 14 affirmations below and affirm your mate twice a day for the next seven days.**

1. _____

2. _____

3. _____

4. _____

5. _____

6. _____

7. _____

8. _____

9. _____

10. _____

11. _____

12. _____

13. _____

14. _____

Chapter 4

How Do I Move Beyond the Hurt and Pain and Start Over?

This may sound silly, but moving beyond the hurt and the pain and starting over is as simple as making a decision to do so. Decide today that you are going to move forward and not look back. The reason why you are going to make a decision to move forward and not look back is because looking back and continuing to trudge up the past over and over again is not in the best interest of the marriage, nor is it in your best interest. I liken it to cutting open a wound that would naturally heal on its own if you did not continue to cut it open over and over again. I am not minimizing your hurt or your pain, but I am pleading with you to forgive your mate and forgive yourself for the errors that have been made in the relationship. In Isaiah 43:25, God made a reference to forgiving Israel, who had sinned against him and hurt him over and over again. God said, "I, *even* I, *am* he that blotteth out thy transgressions for mine own sake, and will not remember thy sins" (KJV). When God says He will not remember their sins, He is saying he will not bring their sins up again. That is what forgiveness is. Sure, we remember what our mate did to us, and we remember what we did to our mate, but true forgiveness is not bringing it up again. After it has been discussed, it is time to move forward.

Wipe the slate clean. Focus your attention on treating your mate the way that God treats you and me. When we sin, we ask for forgiveness, and He welcomes us back into His loving arms. He does not mistreat us upon our return. He does not put us in a holding pattern for His forgiveness and make us work to fully earn it. In fact, He treats us as well as the prodigal son was treated when he returned home (Luke 15:11-32). It may be tough to walk this out, but remember that walking this out is not just about your mate, it's not just about your marriage, it is also about your commitment to God. Do you desire to be like Christ and respond like Christ? Are you serious about your love walk? Will you allow God to use this experience to build your endurance and character? Rebounding at the crossroads and moving beyond the hurt and the pain will test you, but if you allow it to, it will also strengthen you. In Romans 5:3-4, Paul encourages us to rejoice and be strengthened through tough times: "We rejoice in our sufferings, knowing that suffering produces endurance, and endurance produces character, and character produces hope" (ESV). There is hope for this marriage if you are willing to make some adjustments. I am asking you to make adjustments not because I am not of the belief that your mate may also need to make some adjustments, but knowing that you have no control over your mate. Ask God to heal you where you hurt. Ask God to take your focus off of the pain and buffer the intensity of the offense. He will do it! He did it for me, so I know He will do it for you.

When one person in a relationship changes the way he or she thinks and does things, that person alone can change the trajectory of the relationship. For example, if you are playing chess with another individual, your moves alone change the way the game is played and therefore have an impact on the outcome of the game. We oftentimes get to the crossroad and realize that we are wounded and broken in some way. Whether the wounds and brokenness are related to the relationship or not isn't relevant. What is relevant is that it is time to move beyond the hurt and the pain and move in the direction of wholeness. If you feel yourself flooded with emotions, tired, weary, hurt, and perhaps carrying the burdens of yesterdays, allow the crossroad to be a resting station for you to stop, regroup, and focus on becoming all that God created you to be. Take your focus off the relationship for now and focus on you and God. Focus on your relationship with Him. Focus on becoming the best you He intended for you to become. Imagine what that looks like for you.

For me, regrouping and refocusing looked like this: I found a quiet place in my home. I got a blanket, and I laid it out on the floor. Daily, I lay on my face on top of that blanket, and I talked to and listened to God. I asked God to restore in me a clean heart, help me to see people the way He sees them, and help me to look more like Him. I commanded back everything the enemy had stolen from me over the years. I wanted my compassion for others back, my respect for myself back, and my commitment to honor God above my own needs back. I asked God to tame my tongue and help me to make it useful for blessing people and not cursing them. The more time I spent with God, the clearer I was able to see who I had become over the years, and I simply did not like the person I had become. Before spending so much time with God, I had been measuring myself up against my mate, and I thought I looked pretty good. But when I began to really look at who I had become and the pain I had caused those around me, I was ashamed. I saw a wounded person who was okay with wounding other people. My committed time with God helped me to shed the wounds and the shame. God restored me, He strengthened me, He renewed me. I moved beyond the hurt and the pain to a fresh start. And in my newness, I was no longer willing to be the cause for other people hurting. This time with God was not about my husband. It was about me becoming more like God.

During my time alone with God, I learned that reaping and sowing are real. Many of us want the pain to stop. We want to walk away from our brokenness, and we can. In doing so, we must also be willing to look deep within. Take a look at all of the relationships in your life. Are you kind to the people with whom you are in relationship? When I first graduated from U of M with a Master's degree in Social Work, I landed a job right away, and I loved the work, but one of my peers on that job was beyond mean to me. I remember praying and praying for God to remove me or her, but He allowed me to endure in that workplace for a bit before removing me. Looking back, I realize that what she did to me, I was doing to others, and I had not repented. For some reason, I was not able to tie the two together. Now I clearly understand that what I put out into the atmosphere, I welcome back to me. In order for me to move away from the hurt and the pain and start all over again, I had to also walk away from old behaviors and decisions that welcomed hurt into my life. The scripture clearly states in Galatian 6:7, "Be not deceived; God is not mocked: for whatsoever a man soweth, that shall he also reap" (KJV). Maybe you are one of those rare people who has never hurt your mate. Dig deeper. Have you hurt others? Is it possible that the pain that you are distributing is somehow finding its way back to you? I am clearly not saying that if you hurt someone else you deserve to be hurt, because that is simply not true. What I am stating is that in order to truly move away from the hurt and the pain, we must also stop distributing it. We have no control over the choices that others make to harm the innocent. Unfortunately, innocent people are harmed every day, but we get to choose whether we want to partake in causing hurt and pain. Moving beyond the hurt and the pain is a total commitment to be like Christ, to trust Christ to protect us and be kind to everyone we come in contact with. Moving away from the hurt and the pain begins our process of healing from the inside out and sharing genuine love, peace, and harmony with everyone we meet.

You have the power to create a pain-free environment. It starts with you. Creating a pain-free environment starts with your commitment to respect all human beings regardless of their title, rank, or position. Smile at strangers, be kind to loved ones, and by all means, cut off or limit your time with people who bring negativity, gossip, and confusion into your life. Be intentional about being a better you. As a result of my decision to move beyond the hurt and the pain to a new start, my husband wanted to spend more time with me in the pain-free environment that I created. He enjoyed not having to relive the hurt and the pain that I continued to trudge up and question him about over and over again. He was pleased to no longer be the target on whom I used to work out all of my childhood and womanhood issues. For many years, I projected the trauma I observed in relationships as a child into our marriage. He was suddenly pleased to be greeted by me with a smile and loving, kind words instead of suspicion and a snarl. Quite frankly, moving beyond the hurt and the pain was even more rewarding for me because I was able to consciously make a decision to stop carrying all the baggage I had carried for so long. Most of the baggage did not even belong to me. It was my parents' stuff, my aunts' stuff, and many of my friends' stuff. I had allowed it to become mine and impact my relationships. I felt free as a bird when I made a decision to just let it all go and move forward.

You can make a decision today to move away from the hurt and pain and start over with a new perspective on life. Psalm 1:13 states, "Blessed is the one who does not walk in step with the wicked or stand in the way that sinners take, or sit in the company of mockers, but whose delight is in the law of the LORD, and who meditates on his law day and night. That person is like a tree planted by the streams of water, which yields its fruit in season and whose leaf does not wither— whatever they do prospers" (NIV). The new perspective is really about living a life that is pleasing to God by separating yourself from responding in a way that is pleasing to the world. It is also about watching the company that you keep and not allowing yourself to get pulled into speaking or responding like the world. Plant yourself in the word of God and watch God do some amazing things in your life. God has promised to prosper you for your obedience unto Him. When you are living a prosperous life, it's impossible to be sad, depressed, and consumed with what your mate is or isn't doing to please you. I believe that the prosperity that God gives you will attract your mate back to you. If I am wrong, just know that God is more than what you need. Start today. Make a decision to move beyond the hurt and the pain.

1. **What painful experiences am I holding onto and allowing to impact my marriage?**

_____

_____

_____

2. **Lord, I give all the following hurts, pains, and memories over to You because they no longer serve me. I declare that I am healthy—mentally, physically, and spiritually. I will no longer carry the following baggage:**

_____

_____

_____

3. **I will commit myself to being kind, loving, and helpful to everyone with whom I come in contact. I declare that my mate and others will be kind toward me.**

God, What's Next for Me
at The Crossroad?

Chapter 5
Will Divorce End All of the Pain? ("I Want Out")

At the crossroad, things become hot, heavy, and emotionally charged. Many times, it is the weight of the hurt and the pain that pushes one mate or the other in the direction of wanting to get a divorce. Most people do not marry with the thought of getting a divorce in the future. But again, 40 to 50 percent of the U.S. population married for the first time is opting to get a divorce when they encounter a crossroad experience. What is more alarming than that statistic is that the divorce rate in the church is as high as the divorce rate outside of the church. In fact, it is rumored that atheists have a lower divorce rate than Christians. Why are Christians choosing divorce? Because Christians want the pain that brought them to the crossroad to

stop! Many times, our response is emotional and im-
pulsive, and we don't allow God or His word to be a
part of our decision-making process. The desire to get
away from the intensity or pain sometimes causes our
memory to fail us, and we forget that God is a burden
bearer and a heavy load sharer. I Corinthians 10:13
says, "No temptation has overtaken you except what
is common to mankind. And God is faithful; he will
not let you be tempted beyond what you can bear. But
when you are tempted, he will also provide a way out
so that you can endure it" (NIV). The temptation at the
crossroad to get a divorce is certainly common to mankind. But God is faithful, and He gives us the ability to
endure and escape the pain.

I am an optimist, and I love the institution of marriage
that God has put in place. I am for marriage. Many people
do not agree with my perspective on who it takes to make
a marriage work. I believe that it only takes two to get
a marriage back on track at the crossroad. And I do not
mean the husband and wife. The two I am referring to are
God and one willing spouse. The argument from others
is, "Well, God gave us free will, and you can't change a
person's will. We all get to choose." My response is, "God
is the potter, we are the clay, and God allows His will to
override our will daily." As a biblical example, Saul's will
was changed on the road to Damascus and he became
Paul—the person God created and purposed him to be.
What He did to change Paul to become a better person, He

can and will do for each of us. If He did it then, He will do it now. God can override your mate's will and align your mate's will with His will. God still speaks to His children today, and when he speaks, things happen. Change takes place.

When the Israelites were led out of the promise land by Moses, God hardened Pharaoh's heart. God is one who can harden and soften hearts. He can soften the heart of your partner. Trust Him to do it for His glory. God is for marriage. Divorce is not the immediate answer. God is. The scripture says, "Therefore put on the full armor of God, so that when the day of evil comes [crossroad moment], you may be able to stand your ground, and after you have done everything, to stand" (Ephesians 6:13, NIV). Do not make a sudden decision to divorce, because divorce has not been proven to make the pain go away. In fact, after speaking with many couples, I believe it has proven to intensify, and in many cases extend, the pain for many years to come. Many times, we impulsively ask for a divorce, and soon after, we desire to work things out, but the ego gets in the way of repentance, and we believe we have gone too far to retract our decision.

My perspective on the fact that it takes two to get your marriage back on track will work if God is for your marriage. God is for marriages that He put together. He wants married couples to be equally yoked (II Corinthians 6:14). He does not approve of Christians marrying heathens or unbelievers (Deuteronomy 7:3). You are asking for a lot of trouble when you marry against the will of God. His will cannot be overridden by your will. So you must ask yourself, "Did God tell me to marry my mate?" This is important because scripture says what God has put together let no man separate. If God did not put it together, and you or your mate are unwilling to confess the Lord as savior and submit to the marriage operating God's way, you have an extra-long road ahead. It is difficult to bring order into a relationship that God has not ordained. But God is such an awesome God that at any moment, the two of you can make a decision to confess Him as your savior. At that moment, He becomes for you, and He will join you in your union to Him and each other. When you and your mate commit to Him, He becomes for your marriage. There is no problem too difficult for God.

It is unfortunate that men and women today desire so much to be married that they marry the first person who comes along and makes promises to them. Let me say this: couples that God purposed to be together go through the fire, so you better believe that those who think they can do it on their own without God will get burned up. The divorce rate is at 40 to 50 percent for couples in and outside of the church because saved uncommitted couples and unsaved couples refuse to submit their marriage unto God and apply kingdom principles when faced with adversity.

Regardless of how or why you got together, if you are for God, He is for your marriage, and divorce cannot and will not make the pain go away. As a therapist, I have met many divorced women who reconciled in their mind that divorce was the only answer to easing the pain and misery of being married. Over 50 percent of those women with whom I have conversed have stated that they are still miserable and that maybe, just maybe, they should have sought God for relief of the pain that continues to nag on year after year as they mourn the loss of what could have been. They often contemplate about what things would be like if they had just waited on the Lord and not made a rash decision to get out so quickly in search of relief that can only be found in a relationship with God.

Whether you decide to stay in the marital union or leave the marital union, please know that God and only God is the healer of wounds. I have sought Him for myself, and He has healed my heart and restored my soul. I have experienced pain that felt deep and impenetrable, and yet God reached in and healed the pain. The pain of breaking a covenant leaves an open wound because according to scripture, when the two become one, spiritually, you become bone of bone and flesh of flesh (Genesis 2:23). I believe the things of the spirit are more real than the things in the natural. Therefore, when you make a decision to divorce, the two of you are literally tearing apart bone and flesh. In the natural, if you tear apart bone and flesh, pain quickly results. Because the things of the spiritual world are more real than the things of the natural world, we feel the pain of divorce. Again, in the spirit, divorce is a ripping apart of bone and flesh. This results in bleeding and excruciating pain that masks itself in the physical as brokenness. This brokenness is shared with everyone to whom we are connected, including our children if that is applicable. A healing process is necessary so that we do not allow our brokenness and the generational curse of divorce to become contagious among our loved ones.

Meditation:

1. Find a quiet space where you can be alone take your Bible with you.
2. Close your eyes. Take a deep breath in. Now exhale slowly. Repeat that 10 times.
3. Turn to John 10:10b: "I have come that you may have life and have it more abundantly."
4. Close your eyes and repeat John 10:10b in your mind while visualizing what an abundant life looks like for you and your mate. See the two of you involved in doing things together that represent an abundant life.
5. Thank God for healing you, your mate, and your marriage and ordering your steps moving forward.

. . . .

Prayer:

God, I submit this marriage unto You. I submit my will unto You. God, I want what You want for me and this marriage. God, I commit myself to submitting to Your biblical order in the marriage. Lord, I trust You to guide my mate to walking strongly and confidently in godly purpose. Father God, I pray that You allow Your anointing to fall fresh on me and my mate daily. I pray that my mate and I will have a desire to seek after You daily. I pray, Lord, that my mate and I will yearn for Your presence and Your word daily. I pray that You will give me and my mate the supernatural ability to see each other the way that You see us. Lord, I thank You for seeing us and creating us with purpose in mind. Lord, I thank You for being a healer and taking away the pain. Help me to keep my mind on You so that I can experience Your perfect peace. Amen.

Chapter 6
What Am I to Do If My Mate Wants a Divorce?

First of all, scripture declares that if God be for you, who can be against you? (Romans 8:31). God ordained the institution of marriage, and He said that what He put together, let no man separate (Mark 10:9). What I request you to do is trust in the Lord with all your heart. Lean not to your own understanding. Acknowledge Him, and He shall direct your path (Proverbs 3:5-7). Gird up, my friend. Put on your spiritual armor and declare war against the enemy. Get laser-focused on defeating the enemy (the enemy, not your mate).

I know for a fact that I am purposed to decrease the divorce rate by preaching, teaching, and walking with couples and families, helping them to see and use the spiritual weapons God has made accessible to all saints. I am a soldier in God's army, and my mission is to be instrumental in overthrowing the enemy's plan to destroy families through divorce and generational curses. I had been doing just that for over 10 years, and then BOOM! My marriage came under attack. I can't say I was surprised. The enemy came to kill, steal, and destroy. I guess he wanted to test my commitment to the ministry that God purposed me to walk in. Believe it or not, my first response was devastation. I thought, "God, how could You allow this to happen to us? What is going on?" I went to the book store looking for books written by Christians that would give me step-by-step instructions riddled with the word of God on how to prevail against adversity. I was not able to find what I was looking for. The result of that experience is this book.

I got in my closet. I cried, I begged, and I sobbed all over the place. Then I started talking to my husband. I begged him to be restored in our marriage. I whined, I prophesied to him, and I made love to him like never before. Finally, I got a breakthrough. My husband heard me. My tears and my words convinced him that he should be reconciled unto me. A few months passed. I went into relaxation mode and took a few steps back from seeking God daily and spending intimate time with him in prayer. Then BOOM! My husband started looking at me funny all over again. I thought, "Oh my goodness, now what's wrong?" I repented, I begged, I cried, and I said, "I gave you more good sex than ever before. What is your problem?" Then I was back in God's face like, "Okay, God. Why me?" He responded as He often does. "Why not you? He immediately revealed to me that we would experience victory through my patience. He also revealed to me that I needed to walk out what I had been preaching and teaching over the years. I often told couples I counseled that it takes two to make the marriage work: one of you and God. The other person will catch up. The writing was on the wall. God was preparing me for the next level He was going to take me to in the marriage ministry in which He purposed for me to labor.

This second time around, as I stood at the crossroad, things were clearer. This time at the crossroad, I was intent on doing things differently because I did not want to be back at the crossroad in a few months. Please note that I am not discouraging you from crying at the crossroads, and yes, I cried again the second time around, but I understood better that although crying feels good, it did not break any strongholds. Tears are not spiritual weapons, and to my dismay, neither was that good ole extra sex I gave my husband last time we were at the crossroad. Never should we deny our husbands, but wives be clear, it is *not* a spiritual weapon. It may soothe and bring about some temporary relief, but it does not thwart the enemy's plan against your marriage. God showed me that I was back at the crossroads a few months later fighting for my marriage because I thought that the enemy had packed up and went home because my husband was being a sweetheart again. But I had not seen a white flag from the enemy. In fact, I had not really put up much of a fight between talking to my husband, spending more time whining, crying, and talking to my girlfriends, and doing you know what else (giving him something he could feel).

So now a few months had passed, and to my surprise, the enemy had been fighting against our marriage over the past three months. I had been asleep while he was making plans to destroy our marriage and set up generational curses. I had decreased prayer down to some brief time in my closet maybe a couple times a week, and yes, I was back to ignoring my husband and subtlety dishonoring him here and there. So when the enemy reared his ugly head again, it was obvious to me that he had been fighting all along, and he had picked up steam. One evening, he came at me like a roaring lion as my husband said, "We are going to pay off all of the bills and then go our separate ways." I knew immediately that it was war time. I also knew that it was not my husband, Rev. Eliakim Thorpe, speaking to me, but the enemy himself.

At that moment I told myself, "Girl, gird up! You do not have time to cry. You have been chilling over the last few months, and he has been fighting you by attacking your husband's thoughts. Because the two of you are one, you are under vicious attack." As I looked back over the past couple of months, I chuckle as I recall seeing this weird look in my husband's eyes and changes in his tone and extreme moodiness. I chuckle because now I know my husband does not have a man period. Those were manifestations of a satanic attack on him. And yes, I can chuckle, because now that the enemy has been identified. I know exactly how to fight, and I can smile because Jesus is my defense.

Pardon me as I become transparent. I am from the hood, born and raised. If I don't know anything else, I know when and how to fight. See, where I am from, if another chick approaches you with her fist balled up, you already know there is no time for talking or crying. It is time to fight. When the enemy spoke through my husband and said, "We are going to pay off all of our bills and then go our separate ways," he sucker-punched me right between the eyes. But I woke up quickly, and I began to fight with a vengeance. I did not attack my husband. I went directly for the enemy.

The first thing I did was call the prayer warriors to whom I am connected. Well, let me preface that. I called the ones in whom I knew I could confide. The ones whom I was pretty sure would keep the information with which I entrusted them confidential. They gave me resources, they encouraged me, and they put our family on their prayer list. The next thing I did was pray throughout my entire house. I blessed every room from the basement up, and I kicked the enemy out with the word of God. Then I walked the perimeter of our home, and I commanded God's blessing and protection over the brick and mortar from rooftop to the basement joists. I set up camp in my office and my closet to seek God daily for direction, to praise Him for the opportunity to be refined, and to, upon my deliverance, help set others free. I knew that this vicious attack would not be in vain. I felt like a soldier in battle. After a few days of warring for my marriage and my family, I began to war for other families. I was intentional about listening to my girlfriends and church prayer team for opportunities to go to war for them also. I felt like since I was in battle with the enemy and in pursuit of legions, I might as well use the word of God to uproot everything that comes in my direction and in the direction of those God has attached to me. As I prayed the word of God, like James in James 1:2, I began to count it all joy, knowing that the trying of my faith worketh patience, knowing that on the other side of this trial I would be, wanting nothing. I reassured myself that the man who vowed to love me forever did not want a divorce, but the enemy who came to kill, steal, and destroy did want a divorce. I refused to give the enemy what he wanted because I wanted what Jesus wanted for us. He came so that we may have life and have it more abundantly.

So if your mate wants a divorce, you fight for your marriage until the divorce papers are drawn and signed. As you fight the fight with your spiritual weapons, walk by faith and believe that God will turn your mate's heart back to you. You speak things to your mate as though they were. You pray the will of God over your mate. You command the enemy to stop attacking your mate's mind and tell him to flee. You cancel his plan to destroy your marriage in the mighty name of Jesus. Tell the enemy that no weapon formed against your marriage will prosper. In the midst of all of this, seek direction from God and be the person that God created you to be. Focus on growing in the word of God daily and looking and being more like him. I love Mathew 6:33, which says, "But seek ye first the kingdom of God, and his righteousness; and all these things shall be added unto you" (KJV). These things include peace, unity, solidarity, and happiness in your marriage.

I know that holding on to what another person says they do not want can be tiring. Remember, this is how your mate feels right now. Emotions change, but love lasts into eternity. Thomas A. Edison said, "Our greatest weakness lies in giving up. The most certain way to succeed is always to try just one more time."

1. While you are in battle for your marriage, set aside time with God daily for instruction. Seek Him about your every move: what to say, how to say it, patience, and protection from the enemy's darts that will come at you through your mate.

2. Determine in your mind to be kind to your mate, and don't allow the enemy to pull you into a negative space with your mate regardless of what is said or done.

3. Stay focused on the Lord. Depend on Him to protect your heart and guide you.

4. Do not project your pain onto your mate. Run to your closet if you need to and just tell God all about it. Ask God to fix it. Acknowledge that He is in control of your mate.

5. Ask God to soften your mate's heart and turn it back to you.

6. Make up your mind to walk in the peace that surpasses all understanding, even the midst of this adversity.

7. Pray for your friends' and family members' marriages and their needs.

8. Set aside some time to give of yourself in the community to a family or an organization that is in need of volunteers.

9. Declare healing and reconciliation over your marriage. Be persistent and patient and don't give up.

10. Hold your mate's hands if given the opportunity to do so and say, "I love you, and I am thankful that you are my mate."

Prayer:

Lord, I believe that no weapon formed against our marriage will prosper. I declare that my mate and I will be on one accord, and we will prosper together and fulfill the plan that You have for us in the mighty name of Jesus.

Chapter 7
Through the Fire and the Water

There are some things that the enemy knows about us from watching us generation after generation. One thing I imagine he knew about me is that I had processed many of my childhood and adult experiences as rejection and that there was a lot of pain and hurt surrounding my feeling of being rejected. Early in our marriage, I wore rejection like a badge that justified my actions to protect myself. As a result of that, I made a lot of mistakes in our marriage. I cocooned my heart, and I only allowed my husband to get so close. The more I allowed him access to my heart, the more I hurt him in fear of being hurt. I can image that the enemy was waiting for the day to use the mistakes I made in our marriage against me and for an opportunity to convince my husband that he should reject me. Unfortunately, he received his opportunity, and the rejection I felt from my husband was hurtful. It felt like much more than I could endure. I was so overwhelmed with the pain that there were moments when I felt like I could not catch my breath. I would think, "How dare the person who has vowed to love me, cherish me, and forsake all others for me until death do us part reject me?"

Well, the conclusion is that he did not. The truth is that he was hurting as much as I was. There was some generational stuff assigned to him as a child that he had not been able to break away from as an adult. He had not had much of a gap between being the caretaker of his younger siblings under the rule of a very authoritative mom to being the caretaker of our family under the rule of another very authoritative woman—me. As he matured into a man and really came into his own from a spiritual standpoint, the man he was becoming rejected the woman I was. When this happened, I felt rejected.

I felt like my head was being held under water and I could hardly breath. I knew at that moment that in order for this marriage to live, something had to die. Now, as I look back, I can see the image of my then-self fighting to live, fighting against the currents that were keeping me submerged under that water, unable to take a breath but wanting to get through this marital storm, wanting to survive, without making any adjustments. I see my then-self fighting to survive as I was, full of hurt, pain, and rejection that I often projected onto my husband. I can clearly recall the image of myself crying, begging, screaming, and gasping to hold on to the me who contributed to us being in this awful place. All I wanted in that moment was to fight for things to stay the same. I wanted so badly for him to give me permission to continue to be the wounded woman that I was. I wanted his permission to continue to hurt and reject him in order to buffer the pain from the rejection of my past. He refused, and I so I went above him and I pleaded with God to please fix our marriage without me having to change. And God gently showed me the wounded woman I was. He showed me who I had become and I how I had become her, and then He revealed to me who I really was. He revealed to me the character of the person/wife He created me to be. He showed me Isaiah 43:1-2, and God said, "Fear not: for I have redeemed thee, I have called *thee* by thy name [Kimberly]; thou *art* mine. When thou passest through the waters, I *will be* with thee; and through the rivers, they shall not overflow thee: when thou walkest through the fire, thou shalt not be burned; neither shall the flame kindle upon thee" (KJV). I felt comfort in the word of God, and I hung onto it like one would a worn teddy bear. I allowed the then-me to be overwhelmed by the water that she was fighting all around her to stay alive and be burned up by the fire that consumed her desire to continue to fight instead of surrender. But God called the me that He created me to be by name. He called me to surrender to Him, and therefore to my husband. He redeemed me from a life of hurt, pain, and rejection. He walked with me and he bridled my tongue. He clothed me with love, gentleness, and kindness. I continue to have moments when I want to lash out at my husband, then God reminds me of who I am. I am no longer the wife who desires to hurt my husband with my words or defend myself when I feel he is wrong. I have surrendered every battle that I face in this marriage to the Lord. Those times when I am tempted to allow my flesh to rule, I recall I Corinthians 10:13: "There hath no temptation taken you but such as is common to man: but God *is* faithful, who will not suffer you to be tempted above that ye are able; but will with the temptation also make a way to escape, that ye may be able to bear *it*" (KJV). So when I am tempted, instead of allowing my tongue to do what it did for so many years, I close my mouth and smile. If the temptation begins to bubble on the inside of me, and it is almost unbearable to hold in, I run out of the room to my quiet place and start a conversation with God in order to keep from opening my big mouth and wounding my husband.

1. Identify generational curses that have plagued your family.

_____

_____

_____

2. Search yourself for any old emotions you may be holding onto and projecting onto your mate.

_____

_____

_____

3. Ask God to show you your mate's heart and anything that you may need to be more sensitive to concerning emotions your mate may be holding onto from the past and projecting onto you.

_____

_____

_____

Praise God for not allowing the adversity to overtake you. Repeat below:

- God is my strength.

- I am strong.

- I love my mate.

- My marriage is forever.

- We will overcome.

- No weapon formed against this marriage will prosper.

- I declare love, peace, intimacy, prosperity, and trust in our marriage

Prayer:

God, please expose what needs to be uprooted in me. Help me to look, act, and speak more like You. Thank You for being a God who loves me in spite of my flesh, and thank You for maturing me in your word. Thank You for never leaving me or forsaking me. Thank You for always meeting me where I am and elevating me to where You want me to be. I appreciate Your grace and mercy that is extended to me daily. Please bless me with a strong desire to extend grace and mercy to my mate and all others around me. Help me to be considerate and sensitive to the needs of my mate. Help me, Father, to deny myself as I follow You. Thank You for sustaining us through it all and blessing us with joy and peace that surpasses all understanding. Amen.

Chapter 8
Does God See Me?

I have had the privilege of walking with many women and men during their crossroad experiences. I have seen the pain of this moment pierce so deep that many began to ask themselves, "Does God see me? Does He know how much pain I am in?" I have personally known the pain to be so intense that you just feel like you want to run. You want out simply because you want the pain accompanied with this union to just go away. Unfortunately, 40 to 50 percent of the married population runs (divorce). Many times, emotions are high, things are just not going their way, and they are not sure how to navigate. Running away is no new phenomenon. It can be traced back to biblical times. In Genesis 16:1-15, Hagar was having a difficult time being married to Abram. She could not talk to Abram about her issue with his first wife Sarai because Abram gave Sarai authority over Hagar. The relationship between the three of them became so intense and emotionally charged that Hagar made a decision to run. When she ran, the Lord sent his angel to meet her near a spring in the dessert. Hagar initially made a decision to run and not turn back, but God spoke to her through the angel and told her to go back and submit to her mistress Sarai. I'm sure you are thinking, "What? Why would God instruct her to go back and submit to a mistress who is mistreating her?" Your answer is in verse 4: "He (Abram) slept with Hagar, and she conceived. When she (Hagar) knew she was pregnant, she began to despise her mistress" (NIV). In verse 5, Sarai states that she was suffering wrong from Hagar. What God was requiring of Hagar as he instructed her to submit was to look at herself, take responsibility for her behavior, and make some adjustments. Initially, Sarai was obviously fond of Hagar because she chose her to be her baby's momma. According to scripture, their relationship changed after Hagar realized that she was pregnant, and she began to despise Sarai. To simplify it, Hagar was given the task of taking responsibility for her actions as it related to her relationships with her mistress and her husband. Hagar had some work to do, and it started with her first submitting to the authority over Sarai.

In a Christian home, the husband is the authority, and submission is sometimes interpreted as a very nasty word. Many times, once we move past the honeymoon stage in our marriage, we are faced with the reality of a need for order in our home. The foundation of order in a Christian home is authority and submission. The Bible teaches us to submit to God and to each other, but it also teaches us that the husband is the final authority in the home. What does that mean? This means that as the two of you live life together, there will be times when the two you do not agree with moving in the same direction concerning an issue. The husband's responsibility is to listen to his wife's point of view with understanding. The wife's responsibility is to step back and submit to the fact that God has given the husband authority to make the final decision regarding the direction in which the couple will move.

As a wife, this was previously a challenge for me. Like Eve in the Garden of Eden, I wanted to be the final authority. I wanted to sway my husband to do what I wanted him to do when I wanted him to do it. When things did not go my way, instead of seeking God, I wrestled with the urge to just run like Hagar. During our second biggest crossroad moment, I actually visualized packing bags, getting the kids out of bed in their pajamas, piling them up in the car, and beating my husband to the bank to clean out the bank accounts. As I was preparing myself to move forward with my plan, God began to speak to me. He said, "Go to your husband, hold his hand, and ask him to pray with you." My initial response was "What?" Then I said, "Okay, Lord." I did just what he instructed me to do, and God fixed it. That night, my husband and I went to the basement and prayed. We repented to God and each other. As God continues to draw both of us nearer to him, there is more and more to fix.

That experience was one of the first times I was able to hear God speak to me clearly with instruction. Like what happened to Hagar, this was my confirmation that God sees me. God sees me in the midst of my pain, He sees me in the midst of my wrong, He sees me when I feel like no one else can see me. He saw me when things became so bad in my marriage that I contemplated running. Not only did He see me, He called me nearer to Him. He comforted me, and He fixed it. At that crossroad, He fixed me and He fixed us.

We serve a God who sees us. You do not have to suffer in silence. It is not your responsibility to fix yourself, nor is it your responsibility to fix your marriage. Making things right is the responsibility of the God who sees you. He is waiting for you to come and talk to Him. Ask Him for help. What I love most about God is that He knows us to the core of who we are because He is our creator. Therefore, you can go to Him just as you are. With your permission, He will show you the walls, the façade, and disingenuous characteristics you may have taken on knowingly and unknowingly. He will peel back layer after layer and expose the person He created you to be. In exchange for you allowing this process to occur, He promises to be everything you thought those walls and façade were. He has promised to be with you and to protect you while you focus on just being who He created you to be. According to the

Book of Genesis in the Bible, He created you in his image. So you were created to be everything that you know Him to be. God is kind, loving, forgiving, thankful, and gracious. We all become things that God is not in an effort to protect ourselves from being hurt. We build up walls and we live behind façades to protect ourselves. Now that you are at the crossroad, it is time to shed that stuff and allow God to be your protection. He sees you. He knows what you need, and He knows who you are.

This crossroad experience is your opportunity to live authentically. This is your opportunity to no longer allow your mate, the world, or your experiences to shape who you are. You are free today to be who God created you to be. He sees the real you. He wants you to be that person He created you to be, draw you nearer to Him, and have you submit to the authority He has put in place. You are not at this crossroad alone. God has your back. Seek Him for everything he wants you to gain from the crossroad experience.

I came out of my last crossroad experience less focused on my mate and what I thought he should or should not do and more focused on God and my commitment to be who He created me to be. I am committed to being kind, loving, thankful, and forgiving toward all of mankind, not just my husband. I am a better person than I was prior to my crossroad experience. I am like Christ, created in His image. I am relying on God to protect and shield me from people who want to hurt me as I endeavor on the journey to be like Him. Yes, I have experienced some disappointment while on this journey, but God has strengthened me through it and guarded my heart. I trust Him, and I refuse to go back to being the person I was before the crossroad. My mate loves the person I have become for the sake of Christ. My friends and family also love this person God always intended for me be. Most important of all, God sees me, and He is pleased.

Exposing the Lies the Enemy Has Told You about Who You Are:

1. I am <u>kind</u>, NOT <u>mean.</u>
2. I am <u>loving,</u> NOT <u>hateful.</u>
3. I am <u>giving,</u> NOT <u>stingy.</u>
4. I am _____, NOT _____.
5. I am _____, NOT _____.
6. I am _____, NOT _____.
7. I am _____, NOT _____.
8. I am _____, NOT _____.
9. I am _____, NOT _____.
10. I am _____, NOT _____.

"By the grace of God I am what I am."
- I Corinthians 15:10a (NIV)

Prayer:

Thank You, Father, for creating me in Your image. Thank You for seeing me and knowing. Thank You for loving me and feeding me with knowledge and understanding about who You created me to be. Thank You for stripping me of all the masks that I have picked up along the way and walking with me as I strive to live an authentic life for You and in You. Thank You for blessing my mate to be supernaturally attracted to who You created me to be. Thank You for allowing my light to shine so brightly that people around me want to know more about You. Most important of all, thank You for being a God who sees me. Lord, I love you.

Who I Am in Spite of the

Crossroad Experience?

Chapter 9

Why Is Pushing Through the Pain Important?

No one, I mean no one, really wants to go through pain, trials, or discomfort. Even Jesus wanted to turn back. In Luke 22:42, on his way to suffering at the cross, he said, "Father, if you are willing, please take this cup of suffering away from me. Yet I want your will to be done, not mine" (NLT). Aren't you glad he pushed through the pain, the trial, and the discomfort? I am, because it produced the gift of eternal life. Jesus obeyed God, and the trials that he experienced produced great reward and increase. It is no different for us when we experience trials. If we obey God through the trial, the result will produce great rewards.

When I think about pushing through the pain, I think about childbirth. No matter how much I complained about the invasion of my body, being 30 pounds overweight, and the pain of the labor, the final product was those precious little hands and feet and that beautiful face. I learned through that experience that even though the pain and trials were not wanted, they were responsible for producing something good.

If or when you experience a crossroad moment in your marriage, know that the trial, pain, and discomfort can produce something good. Trials are designed to produce greatness. The Book of James says, "Consider it pure joy, my brothers and sisters, whenever you face trials of many kinds, because you know the testing of your faith produces perseverance. Let perseverance finish its work so that you may be mature and complete, not lacking anything" (James 1:2-4, NIV). After being with my husband for 20 years, I have learned during a trial to take my focus off of the trial and put it on the outcome. I know without a doubt that when a trial comes, if I walk it the way that God instructs me to, there is a great reward on the other side of the trial.

We have experienced promotion, enlargement of our territory, and great victories on the other side of every trial we have been through. We are entrepreneurs. About 10 years ago, we sustained a vicious trial just before the door was opened for us to start our second business together. The trial was so weighted that I created a separate bank account and had my money direct-deposited into the separate account in preparation to leave. I heard God speaking to me as I made the calls in preparation to open up a separate account, but I ignored His voice until I no longer could. Finally, I went to my closet and listened to the voice of God. I obeyed God, although I felt justified to leave. I prayed the words He gave me, and as I prayed, He healed the offense. As God was speaking and directing me, He was also speaking to my husband. God immediately gave us an increase because we were faithful with the instruction He gave us to weather the trial. Going through the trial strengthened our union. We needed to be able to walk in obedience and forgiveness in order to access the blessings on the other side of our trial. In hindsight, we would not have been successful with the business He blessed us with if we had been unwilling to hear His voice, respond to His voice, deny our feelings, and obey Him while in the trial. It is important to push through the trial, pain, and discomfort to discover the beauty on the other side of your current situation. There is something great on the other side when we allow God to lead us.

While in the midst of a trial, I am careful to repeat and meditate on the following scripture over and over again: "Trust in the LORD with all your heart, and lean not to your own understanding; In all of your ways acknowledge him, and He shall direct your paths" (Proverbs 3:5-6, NKJV). Depend on the Lord to direct you through the pain in your life. God is a great navigator. If you depend on Him, He will not allow you to be overtaken by your pain. In the midst of my crossroad experiences, I asked God to exchange my pain for His joy, and I began to thank Him for the little things that we often take for granted.

I thank Him for my emotions and the ability to feel joy, love, and pain. I thank Him for being in my right mind and the opportunity to come to Him for help and comfort. I thank Him for my health, my life, and my strength. I thank Him for protecting me from hurt, harm, danger, and disease. Before long, God and I are having a praise session, and my mind is no longer on the pain. Instead, I am joyful because I have a God who sees me, knows me, and understand my needs.

1. Locate a scripture in the Bible that encourages you to push forward beyond adversity.

_____

_____

_____

2. Write about a time in your life when you had to overcome adversity. How did you get through it? Did you experience a blessing after the adversity?

_____

_____

_____

3. List four other couples you will be able to minister to and encourage when you get over the adversity in your marriage.

_____

_____

_____

4. List the names of the people who are rooting for you to push through to victory.

_____

_____

_____

5. Starting today, for the next seven days, I want you to declare victory over the adversity that is before you and your mate. (Meditate on Mark 11:24.) Write down what God speaks to you over the next seven days.

_____

_____

_____

Chapter 10

You Have Been Given the Ministry of Reconciliation. What Are You Going to Do With It?

According to II Corinthians 5:18, we have been reconciled unto God and given the ministry of reconciliation. What does that mean? I believe that it means that I am good with God regardless of the mistakes that I have made in my past and those that I will likely make in the future. Now in my reconciled state, I become an ambassador for God, on the mission to get others reconciled unto him. That is a huge responsibility, but every Christian has been called to do it. The good thing is we do not have to do it alone. We have help. God has promised never to leave us or forsake us.

When I learned this scripture as a babe in Christ, this was a bit hard for me to swallow, and quite honestly, it took me years to walk in it as it relates to marriage. Sure, I was able to lead others to the Lord. God used me to reconcile many of his children back to Him. But what did that really look like at home with me and my husband? As a wife, I had been given the ministry of reconciliation, and yet there were many days when I just simply did not want to be reconciled with my husband. Seriously, no one, I mean no one, can offend you like a mate. I have talked to hundreds of Christian couples. From a fleshly perspective, the offenses vary from, "my mate disrespected me in front of our children" to "my mate had an affair." From a God perspective, it is all reconcilable. We get to decide. Having been given the ministry of reconciliation, we get to decide *how* we will reconcile it, not *if* we will reconcile it. As Christians, we don't get to choose to live unreconciled unto anyone because we have chosen Christ. Many would say we are free moral agents and we have the right to choose. My response is that if you are a Christian, you have chosen. You chose Christ, you chose His word, you chose the ministry of reconciliation, therefore you have chosen to be reconciled unto your mate. Choosing to be reconciled is like choosing life vs death. It's like choosing health vs sickness. Webster's Dictionary defines reconciliation like this: "The act of causing two people or groups to become friendly again after an argument or disagreement." To live life unreconciled of offenses is unhealthy, and quite frankly, will only impact you in a negative way.

If being reconciled is a difficult task for you, I strongly advise you to take that to the Lord in prayer. Those who have a difficult time with reconciliation will attempt to be reconciled or forgive, and then before long, they are triggered by an external or internal incident, and they pick the offense right back up as if it occurred yesterday. Carrying an offense is detrimental to the marriage union. If you are having a difficult time being reconciled to your mate, then God is having a difficult time with you. In Mark 11:25-26, God takes a clear stand on this issue of forgiveness. It is stated, "And when ye stand praying, forgive, if ye have ought against any: that your Father also which is in heaven may forgive you your trespasses. But if ye do not forgive, neither will your Father which is in heaven forgive your trespasses" (KJV). God sent his son Jesus as payment for all sin. Is that not enough?

When I am upset with my husband, I have to stop and ask myself, "What do I want from him?" My first thought is...blood! Just kidding! Seriously, I want him to acknowledge that he has wronged me in some way. The issue is that I can't make him give me what I want, so then I must choose, will I be bitter and unreconciled or reconciled and free. It is my choice. I am a mental health therapist by profession. Therefore, I know that there is plenty of research out there that reveals that being unreconciled to anyone for any reason breeds sickness and disease. It takes a lot of energy to remain in an unreconciled state with anyone. To avoid physical sickness and distress, I choose to forgive my mate immediately when he offends me. Why? Because I refuse to allow him to offend me, hurt me, and make me sick. I have God to help me with being reconciled unto my husband. If the offense seems bigger than me, I take it to God, and He has a way of softening my heart toward my husband beyond my ability to do so.

Although I may make forgiving immediately sound easy, I know it isn't. But I understand that in order to be reconciled unto God, I must be reconciled unto my mate. God has given me the ministry of reconciliation, and I choose to walk in it. Whenever God commands us to do something, He has a responsibility to help us do it. God does not shy away from His responsibility to assist us with being reconciled unto our mates. It is His will. He is a God of reconciliation and restoration. There is no offense too large for God.

I counseled a couple that suffered a huge offense in their marriage. The husband had an affair with his wife's mother. If you will allow me to be transparent, I wanted to smack him in the first counseling session. I was offended, and I was not in a covenant relationship with him. I went into prayer immediately for me, the couple, and her mother. God had to remind me that we do not wrestle against flesh and blood but against principalities, against powers, against the rulers of darkness of this world, against spiritual wickedness in high places. I understand that the husband committed this egregious act, but I cannot overlook the fact that he was certainly under demonic influence. He was remorseful, and he was begging his wife for forgiveness. And she was as offended as you think she should have been. But they were both Christians, and they both knew they were not authorized to stay in a state of unforgiveness. They also understood that if they chose to stay there, they would be choosing to go with the enemy's plan to kill and destroy three generations of relationship. It was the familiar story of one man's sin impacting relationships for generations to come. Although it was clear to them both that they had been given the ministry of reconciliation, they chose not to be reconciled unto one another. The couple made a decision to divorce. The last time I checked in with the husband, he reported total destruction within the family unit. Both remarried, and both are divorced a second time. I am confident that their story would be different today if they had chosen to be reconciled unto one another.

I am sure many of you are thinking that what the husband did was unforgivable. But I disagree. I believe the marital covenant between God, man, and woman is so powerful that there isn't a circumstance that cannot be overcome. I have seen couples push through some really difficult times. I have been amazed by the human spirit's ability to forgive, release, and move forward. If you have indeed married the right person, he or she is worth doing the work to get on the other side of the offense and live a lifestyle of reconciliation.

Again, according to Webster, reconciliation is "the act of causing two people to become friendly again after an argument or disagreement." Choosing to be reconciled unto each other does not mean that the couple I mentioned earlier had to choose to stay married. But it does mean they would have chosen forgiveness, peace, love, and godly co-parenting. Ten years later, they continue to fight concerning the children. Choosing reconciliation means they would have chosen to put the kids' needs and their love for them above their emotions tied to the offense. It also means that they would have been better positioned to walk in the ministry of reconciliation and be instrumental in reconciling others back to Christ. We must be careful not to allow what happens to us in a marital union distract us from purpose. Marriage is great, but we were put here for the purpose of building up the kingdom. We cannot allow the decisions that our mate makes to allow us to become distracted from our purpose here on earth. We who have been given the ministry of reconciliation choose to walk in that calling in spite of what our mate does to offend us. Our purpose is larger than the offense. Be reconciled.

Today I commit to releasing myself from carrying offenses from my mate.

1. I forgive my mate for the following offenses:

_____

_____

_____

2. I forgive myself for the following offenses:

_____

_____

_____

Meditation:

Find a quiet place, and for the next 30 minutes, med-itate. Visualize the shackles falling off of you. Visualize being set free from the judgment of yourself and others. Visualize yourself walking forward free of the weight of unforgiveness that had you bound.

....

Prayer:

Lord, keep me from being distracted from the work that You have for me to do. My desire is to be in Your will and Your will alone. Help me to navigate through the things of this world that attempt to distract me from completing my assignment to live according to

Kimberly Bracewell-Thorpe, LMSW

Your word, build up Your kingdom, and make disciples. Help me to be mindful to respond with forgiveness to offense the way that You respond. Help me to look and respond so much like you that others will desire to have you as their Lord and Savior. Amen.

Chapter 11
God Change Me

As Christians, we are likely to have our life circumstances bring us to a spiritual place in our physical bodies where we begin to feel a need to cry out to God, "Change me, Lord. I desire to look more like You." Many of us get to this place because we are tired of fighting against the will of God for our lives—tired of fighting our spouse, tired of fighting others around us, and tired of fighting ourselves. We realize that we are functioning out of character, and we have no idea how we got to a place where we are willing to compromise our relationship with God in exchange for being able to say and do whatever we want to say and do to our spouse and others in spite of how the Bible has instructed us to love, revere, and cherish our spouse and others. We come to God with a desire to connect with someone who knows us and understands us on an intimate level. Like David, we say, "LORD, You have searched me and known me" (Psalm 139:1, HCSB).

Because God knows us even better than we know our-selves, He is able to usher us into change for the better. When our marriage became very dark and we were con-templating divorce, I began to look to God for my reflec-tion. I wanted to know who I am. My face was in the Bible like one looking in a mirror. I understood that looking at God through His word would expose me and convict me to make the changes I needed to make in order to become who He created me to be instead of who I had become as a result of my experiences. The more I looked at God, the more I wanted to be like Him and the less I wanted to remain the person I had become. As I began to look more and more like God, my husband was drawn to me. If we are not careful, the world has a way of drawing us away from God and our spouse.

I recall going to my secret place and saying, "God, change me. Uproot all the stuff that I have learned and processed over the years that is not of You. God, I want to be more like you. I want to be who You created me to be, married or divorced. Lord, I surrender me and every-thing about me to You. Re-build, re-shape, renew my spir-it, mind, and body." I prayed this prayer, and afterwards, I went through a complete metamorphosis. It started with my heart racing and my body feeling an overwhelming sense of anxiety when my flesh wanted to respond the way that I was accustomed to responding when my hus-band said something that I did not like. It did not take me long to realize that the racing heart and the overwhelming feeling of anxiety meant "Kim, don't speak." I began to obey the small, still voice, and immediately, my entire body became calm, relaxed, and content. I welcomed the testing of my faith and my decision to choose and trust God over and over again. I began to feel good about no longer choosing to fight and instead allowing God to defend me, even when I felt justified in defending myself. Others started to notice that not only had I stopped fighting my husband, I had also stopped fighting the people at the grocery store, the people at other businesses in the community, friends, and family. I realized that it felt good to just not fight and trust God. As he renewed my way of thinking, seeing, processing, and responding, I felt a weight lift from my body, and God continued to remind me that it is his job to go before me to fight my battles. He often reminded me in his word "that if he is for me, who can be against me?" Today, my defenses are down, and I can truly say that I trust God with my marriage. I trust God with my life.

This experience changed me, and it also changed the way that my husband responded to me. I am no longer defensive toward him. He reports that he had no choice but to throw in the towel because there was no one to battle. Within a year of God changing me, I recall my husband lying down next to me and whispering gently in my ear, "I feel like I am falling in love all over again." Of course I responded, "What makes you feel that way?" and he said, "Because you are no longer tense or defensive toward me and ready to fight." We both acknowledge that God changed me, and in doing so, he also changed my husband. Immediately after the whisper, we embraced and rejoiced before God for changing both of us. We laughed about the crossroad we crossed over and the thoughts that we both had that were absolutely contrary to the will of God for us. We rejoiced on the other side of our crossroad, and you can too.

My husband and I realize that this will not be every couple's story. Whether you stay together or separate, God still desires for you to surrender your heart to Him so that you can become more like Him. Surrendering ourselves to God is constant. It is never-ending. Every day that I arise, I acknowledge Him as Lord and I surrender to His will for my life. For me, the surrendering daily is important and necessary because for most of my life, I said and did what I wanted to say and do with no consideration for what the word of God instructed me to do. I did what felt right to my flesh. I did the things that brought my flesh satisfaction and got approval from the world. I used to feel justified in threatening my husband saying, "If I every catch you cheating, I will kill you and her." The sad thing is that he never gave me a reason to accuse him of such actions. I just felt justified in letting him know that I felt like it would be okay for me plead temporary insanity after harming him and some woman I had created in my head. God changed me. I no longer allow the enemy to have that kind of access to my thoughts. As a result of God changing me, like Paul in Galatians 2:20, I have been crucified with Christ. It is no longer I who lives, but Christ who lives in me. And the life I now live in the flesh, I live by faith in the Son of God, who loved me and gave himself for me.

In 2 Samuel 11, David, a married man, committed adultery against his wives and against God. In Psalm 51, David sought God for repentance of that sin. David understood that the most important one he had sinned against was God. David sought God for change. In verse 10, David asks God to "create in me a clean heart, O God, and renew a right spirit within me" (ESV). David understood that many people were hurt as a result of the sin that he committed. He also knew that if he became a changed man before God, that he would be better to those around him. David committed to help others follow God if God restored him (verse 13). When David sought after God to be changed, he got right to the core of the issue at hand—him, his heart, and his spirit. David was honest with God about what he needed God to change in him. We must be honest with God about who we are and surrender to Him the areas we need changed in our life. Then, we must make a commitment to do work for the kingdom, helping others draw nearer to God, starting with our spouse. David said he will sing God's righteousness aloud. David changed his focus from his sin to God. When we change our focus from our sin to God, God changes us. When God changed David, David became a more committed servant and a more committed husband. Scripture does not record David continuing to have adulterous relationships. When we sincerely ask God to change us, He does His part.

When we sin against our spouse, we have also sinned against God. Our first step should consist of seeking God for repentance. True change requires God's help. I wanted to be a better wife, so I sought God. I sought God because I needed the strength to truly change and become a wife with whom God and my husband would be pleased. I repented to my husband for hurting him on many occasions, but there was no change prior to seeking God. I simply did not have the ability to make the changes that I told my husband that I would make before seeking God. The change that I committed to making was simply bigger than me, but certainly not bigger than God.

Meditate on Psalm 51.

Write your own repentance statement to God. Your statement should consist of:

- Your asking God to change you to become more like Him

- Your asking God for grace and mercy concerning the sin you have committed

- Your repenting for the sin you have committed

- Your telling God who you are and how you think you may have gotten to this place and asking God to reveal to you how you got here

- Your being honest with God. Let God know how you want to feel when you are no longer carrying the weight of the sin from which he will release you (e.g., sin against yourself, sin against God, sin against your mate, guilt for accepting less than the will of God for your life).

- Your letting God know what you will do for the kingdom now that you are restored

Write down 5 characteristics you want to be known for exhibiting consistently (e.g., honest, polite, giver, godly, patient)

1. _____

2. _____

3. _____

4. _____

5. _____

How often will you commit to meeting God in your secret place? (daily, weekly, monthly)

_____

Just Me and God

Chapter 12

Being in Relationship with God

If our relationship with our spouse is to become everything that God wants it to be, we must first start with our relationship with God. None of us have arrived as it relates to being close to God. We can all stand to get closer than we are today, even if we think we are in a good place with Him.

Let's start with Romans 10:9: "That if thou shalt confess with thy mouth the Lord Jesus, and shalt believe in thine heart that God hath raised him from the dead, thou shalt be saved" (KJV). What does this confession mean as it relates to the type of spouse you are and the type of spouse God wants you to become?

In order to get to where we want to go, we only need to deal with the very first part of this verse: "If thou shalt confess with thy mouth the Lord Jesus." What does that mean to you? As you agree with this verse, you are saying,

"Lord, I confess that you are the Lord of my life." This confession represents a commitment to God to do things His way and not your own. This is a commitment to live for God according to the word of God.

Now locate yourself in that scripture. Are you living according to the confession that you made with your mouth? I am under the impression that a lot of us play with God and go through the motions as it relates to being a Christian and making that confession. The proof is in the pudding. The divorce rate is 40 to 50 percent in the church. I myself have contemplated divorce. I am not so naive to believe that there are not some exceptions. As Paul alluded to in scripture, some people may need to divorce to keep from catching a case. But the truth is that not every divorce is justified. Many of us are divorcing simply because we have allowed our ego, our flesh, or our selfishness to rule over us and our ability to make sound spiritual decisions about how to navigate at the crossroad.

Christians getting divorced should be an oxymoron. That is, if every Christian is serious about the confession we made in Romans 10:9. Many Christians have said, "Lord, I confess that you are the Lord over my life". Now think about your life and the decisions that you make day to day. Ask yourself, "Do I live a life that reflects that I have given God lordship over my life? Do the people with whom I associate daily know that I am a Christian? Can they tell by the way that I speak, act, and present myself?" God does not want to be hidden. He wants people to know that He is Lord of your life. According to Matthew 10:32-33, "Whosoever therefore shall confess me before men, him will I confess also before my Father which is in heaven. But whosoever shall deny me before men, him will I also deny before my Father which is in heaven" (KJV). What is so amazing about David in Samuel I and II is that he sought God before making decisions. Every time he contemplated making a move, he asked, "God, should I…?" David acknowledged God as his Lord, the Lord over his life, and he lived a life that reflected his commitment to staying in the will of God at all times. Even when it made sense to be vengeful, he sought the will of God instead of succumbing to his flesh. Are you willing to do that in your marriage? Are you willing to seek God and commit to his will even when you and those around you feel like you are justified in retaliating against your mate? Sure, David could have killed Saul over and over again, but he had such respect for Saul's position (king) and God's will that he did not retaliate against a man who was seeking to destroy him. I don't believe your mate is seeking to destroy you, but I am sure that at moments, it feels like it. But like David, in those moments, can you revere and honor your mate for the position (husband or wife) God has put him or her in? At those moments, can you seek God for your next move?

Take a self-assessment of your relationship with God:

- Do I hide my relationship with God?

- Do strangers know that I belong to Him?

- Do I act as an ambassador for God?

- Do I really know God?

- Do I spend time with God?

- Do I surrender my fleshly thoughts to Him?

- Do I meet Him regularly in a secret place and pursue Him?

- Do I get excited about being in His presence?

- Am I a reflection of Him?

- Do I see myself as a servant?

- Do I serve my spouse cheerfully?

- Is my marriage a ministry with which God is pleased?

- Is how I behave in my marriage a reflection of Him?

- Do I trust God to navigate my every move?

- Can I respect the position that God has given my spouse when I feel justified to be vengeful?

- Do I trust God to defend me?

Yes is the answer to all of the questions above if He truly is the Lord over your life. The evidence of His Lordship over your life is His being pleased with you. God is pleased

when we believe that He is Lord and that He is a reward-
er of those of us who diligently seek him (Hebrews 11:6).

In order to be in the right relationship with God, we
must diligently seek Him. Your marriage is not your primary relationship. Your relationship with God is your
primary relationship because you have confessed Him as
Lord over your life. It is not possible to have a great, fulfilling relationship with your spouse if you never spend time
with your spouse, getting to know your spouse, understanding his or her needs or expectations, and becoming
one with your spouse. It is no different with God (the Lord
over your life). It is impossible to have a great, fulfilling
relationship with God if you randomly spend time with
Him or only speak to Him in crowds (at church). If you
never spend intimate, one-to-one time with Him, how do
you truly become one with Him and understand what His
will is concerning you?

Today, I want you to go find a spot in an empty room
and talk to Him. Block everything and everyone else out.
It is just you and Him. Play some soft music if you prefer.
I want you to, begin to talk to Him. Tell Him why you are
before Him right now. Let Him know what is so heavy
on your mind today. Release the things or thoughts that
have separated you from Him. Give Him the thoughts
or actions that you find difficult to control. Pause and listen to Him for direction. The focus of this conversation
is on God and what He wants from you. Give Him the
things and the thoughts that have created a wedge in your

relationship with Him. Give Him the things and thoughts that you have been holding on to. Give Him the things that you have put in His place. Let Him know that you truly want to experience Him being your protector, your God, the Lord over your life. Release yourself of being your protector and your God. Release yourself from being the one on whom you depend when things get tough. He wants that place. Give it to Him.

Write down five things that you released to Him (behaviors, thoughts, actions that stand in the way of God being in his rightful place in your life):

1. _____

2. _____

3. _____

4. _____

5. _____

God is a relational God. Until He is in His rightful place in your life, your life is off balance. We thrust ourselves into these marital relationships subconsciously concluding that the marriage is our primary relationship. We get so distracted with the marital relationship and pleasing our spouse that we forget about God. We put Him on the back burner until we get to a crossroad moment and realize that we need Him. We need Him to not only to be a part of our marriage, but we also need Him to be a part of our everyday life. We need to consult with Him daily on how to be the best "me" each of us can be. We need Him to direct us as we become all that He created us to become. We need Him to direct us concerning our purpose and place in this world. We need Him to direct us concerning the ministry that He has called us to work in. When we come to this realization, we begin to diligently seek Him with all of our heart. It is then that we realize, like the father of the prodigal son, He has been waiting for us to come back to Him. It is at that time that we realize that we are happier in His presence, we are free in His presence, and we are loving in His presence. It is in His presence that we learn how to love our spouse the way that He wants us to love.

We are welcomed into His presence and greatly rewarded with peace that surpasses all understanding. It is in His presence that we find rest. It is in His presence that we feel most loved. It is in His presence that we receive the ability to extend the purest form of love to everyone around us. It is in His presence that we wake up to the truth of understanding that we are simply unable to give to others what we have not pursued and received from Him.

Chapter 13
How to Get in His Presence

"But if from thence thou shalt seek the LORD thy God, thou shalt find him, if thou seek him with all thy heart and with all thy soul."

- Deuteronomy 4:29, KJV

From wherever you are, regardless of your current circumstances, seek God. He does not care what you have done in your past. He does not care what you were planning to do tomorrow. He just wants you to make a decision today to seek Him with your whole heart so that He can be in constant relationship with you. God is not satisfied with a Sunday relationship with you. He wants all of you every day.

God referred to David as a man after his own heart, not because David was perfect, but because David was relational with God. David desired to be in God's presence. David talked to God about his innermost personal thoughts. David sought after God with his whole heart. A great example of David being relational with God is found in Psalm 139:1-24.

Do you think it is useful to have with God the type of relationship that David shared with God? Is being relational with God important to you?

Locate yourself in the following truth and seek God from your current position. "For do I now persuade men, or God? or do I seek to please men? for if I yet pleased men, I should not be the servant of Christ" (Galatians 1:10, KJV)

How different would our lives be if we arose morning after morning intent on seeking the manifest presence of God in our lives? Go to Him each morning seeking His will to be done in your life, not your will. Seek to be a representative of love, extend love, and walk in love because God is love. Would seeking God in this way change who you are?

Some time ago, I saw the movie *Focus*, starring Will Smith as the lead. His character made a living as a con man. He had the ability to steal almost anything off of a person's being, and he trained others to do the same. The one thing that intrigued me about the movie was that as he trained others on how to steal, he impressed upon them the following statement: "Once you have a person's focus, you gain access to everything else" (their purse, wallet, jewelry, etc.). It was amazing what the cons were able to steal off of a person's being while looking the victim directly in the eyes or diverting the victim's focus on something other than what was being accessed. I do not condone stealing, but I loved the message. As I watched the movie, I began to think that God desires to have our focus. Once we give Him our focus, He gains access to everything else: our thoughts, our heart, our attitude, our next step, and how we process and respond to people and our environment. Once we give Him our focus, He receives access to all that we are, and we are never the same. We become more like Him.

How do you plan to show God that He has your focus?

_____

_____

....

Lord, starting today, I surrender my heart, mind, body, and soul to You. I am tired of making all of the decisions. Today, I submit to Your will for my life. I want to hear Your voice, Lord. I want to receive your guidance. I give You access to my every thought. Please order my steps according to Your will. Amen.

Seeking the Presence Of God

Seek his presence and meditate on the following scriptures:

"'Am I a God near at hand,' says the LORD, 'And
not a God afar off? {24} Can anyone hide himself
in secret places, So I shall not see him?' says the
LORD; 'Do I not fill heaven and earth?' says the
LORD.'"

- Jeremiah 23:23-24, NKJV

"Draw near to God, and he will draw near to you.
Cleanse your hands, you sinners, and purify your
hearts, you double-minded."

- James 4:8, ESV

"Let us come before His presence with
thanksgiving; Let us shout joyfully to Him with
psalms. {3} For the LORD is the great God And the
great King above all gods."

- Psalm 95:2-3, NASB

"O taste and see that the LORD is good:
blessed is the man that trusteth in him."

- Psalm 34:8, KJV

Schedule a date with God this week, just you and Him,
and bask in His presence.

Chapter 14

We Were Created to Glorify the Father

Again, as a therapist and ordained ministers, my husband and I have counseled many couples. On more than one occasion, we have led couples to experiencing dramatic improvements in their marital relationships by encouraging them to apply scripture to their everyday lives, specifically concerning how they converse with one another. One of our favorite application scriptures is Ephesians 4:29: "Let no corrupt communication proceed out of your mouth, but that which is good to the use of edifying, that it may minister grace unto the hearers" (KJV). Try applying that scripture during a disagreement and watch how the outcome changes. In other words, God does not want you to say anything to your spouse that does not lift your spouse up and bring grace to the two of you. This scripture prompts couples to transition from focusing on each other's flaws and shortcomings to focusing on being kind and respectful to each other. This does not mean that you cannot express to your spouse your disappointments. You are just called to express yourself in a way that does not demean your spouse. You are commanded to express yourself in a way that will edify your spouse and bring grace to him or her. When we present this scripture to Christian couples and ask them to apply it at all times, the initial unanimous response is, "I feel like I can't tell him or her how I really feel." Our response is, "Yes you can, you just have to do it God's way." The truth is if we have done the work of seeking God with our whole heart for a sincere relationship with Him and submitting to Him, then applying scripture is not as much of a challenge as it would be if we were not in relationship with God and we were not willing to submit to Him. Therefore, if applying scripture and doing things God's way is difficult for you, I challenge you to ask yourself, "Have I submitted myself to God? Do I have a genuine relationship with Him, one that makes my heart desire to please Him?"

There is value in having a partner and being a partner. Don't allow the enemy to steal your identity of being a great husband or a great wife. Your oneness with your mate brings value to the kingdom of God. There is multiplication and duplication power in your oneness. God used Adam and Eve to create many generations. He gave them power and authority to multiply and duplicate. As Christians, our focus should be to duplicate ourselves. There is a difference between multiplication and duplication. Any two people can multiply (have babies, adopt babies, raise children). But God has called Christians couples to also duplicate. "Go therefore and make disciples" (Mathew 28:19, ESV). Duplication is about making disciples for God; teaching others by example how to become disciples of God. If we are doing this thing right, we are to disciple, walk alongside, set an example, and encourage a couple to become more like Christ.

The key to prospering in your marriage is obeying the word of God and being intentional about finding other vessels (couples) and pouring into them. In 2 Kings 4:1-6, the widow woman was impoverished and in need of prosperity. She asked the prophet to assist her so that she would not lose her sons to the debt. The prophet asked her what she had in her home, and she replied oil. Oil is representative of the Holy Spirit in the Bible (article Christian study – Patheos). Like unto the widow woman, God has given us the Holy Spirit as well as the task of going out to seek vessels into which to pour the Holy Spirit. When you find vessels into which to pour the Holy Spirit, as the widow lady did in obedience to the man of God, your marriage will prosper. When we keep our focus on us, we lose or miss out on the blessing of prospering and witnessing our prosperity to others. We are together for no other reason but to do the will of the father, prosper, and duplicate ourselves. When we choose to only focus on ourselves, we lose because we will find faults in one another and allow ourselves to become distracted by one another. God has called us to fellowship with other couples in and outside the body of Christ.

In Acts II, what happened when the people came together, broke bread together, and prayed on one accord? They impacted the kingdom. The kingdom of God experienced duplication and multiplication. If you want to keep the purpose of your marriage in perspective, remember this one thing—the two you were united for no other reason except to build up the kingdom. Making disciples is our primary reason for being here on earth, yet we allow the enemy to distract us with so many unimportant things, like "Who are you talking to?" "Where have you been?" "Where is the money?" "Why are you looking at him or her?" Maybe I shouldn't say the answers to those questions isn't important, because they are, but according to scripture, when we all meet our maker, not one of those questions will be asked. The focus will be "Did you obey the word of God and impact the kingdom? Better yet, did you make disciples? Did you and your spouse work for the kingdom, or were you distracted from kingdom work by the things of this world?"

As we know, the divorce rate is teetering between 40 to 50 percent in and outside of the church. Over 50 percent of the couples I have counseled have experienced infidelity or some type of abuse in the marriage. Locate your marriage in this statistic. As a therapist, I know for sure that most of us fall into one of these categories. Why? Because we have allowed ourselves to be distracted. I want you to say to yourself, "I will no longer allow myself to be distracted." The next statement has to be "I will no longer be distracted because I will be about my Father's business." If you are with your spouse, together say, "We will no longer allow ourselves to be distracted because we are going to be about our Father's business." Being about the Father's business consists of obeying the word of God, living according to purpose, and making disciples.

Let's start by committing to obeying scripture and using scripture to navigate in this marriage.

Scripture #1: Ephesians 4:29-32 (KJV)

> [29] Let no corrupt communication proceed out of your mouth, but that which is good to the use of edifying, that it may minister grace unto the hearers.

> [30] And grieve not the holy Spirit of God, whereby ye are sealed unto the day of redemption.

> [31] Let all bitterness, and wrath, and anger, and clamour, and evil speaking, be put away from you, with all malice:

> [32] And be ye kind one to another, tenderhearted, forgiving one another, even as God for Christ's sake hath forgiven you.

This scripture is certainly a mouthful and a humbling challenge. Keep in mind that living this scripture is not commanded by me or your spouse. Instead, God has commanded that we all live according to this scripture. As a Christian, you are obligated to live according to this scripture. If you are anything like me, you have read this scripture over one hundred times without a thought of applying it to your marriage. I recall this scripture being mere words that sounded pretty good written in the Bible. When I felt that way, it wasn't because I wasn't saved or that I did not know of God. It was because I had not sought a relationship with God. My heart was not focused on obeying Him and pleasing Him. Honestly, I was just going through the motions with God and my husband. But when I began to seek God with my whole heart for a relationship with Him, His word came alive, off the Bible pages, and began to penetrate my eyes and heart more than ever before. I wanted to please God. I wanted to show Him that I love Him and I value this person He gave me. I better understood that I can show God how much I love him and how much I value my spouse by obeying His word. A desire to please your spouse is good, but a desire to please God is even better. When I aim to please God, my husband is always pleased. It's the best two-for-one deal in the whole world.

Starting today, can the two of you focus on a fresh start to please God by obeying His word? Yes, I understand that you may have some unresolved issues. I understand that you may have hurt each other in the past. I understand that things may be so painful right now that it seems easier to just walk away. But guess who understands that even better than I do? God.

Do this for me. Write down all the things your spouse has done to hurt you on a piece of paper.

1. _____

2. _____

3. _____

4. _____

5. _____

6. _____

7. _____

8. _____

9. _____

10. _____

Get it all out. Maybe your spouse lied, cheated, turned his or her back on you, forsook you for others, said things that hurt you, or did not keep his or her word or the vows made to you. Now, I want you to look at that list you made and ask God, "Lord, have I ever done any of these things to you?"

1. Lord, have I ever lied to You?
2. Lord, have I ever cheated on You by allowing other people or things to become my God?
3. Lord, have I ever turned my back on You and sought after the things that my flesh craved?
4. Lord, have I always kept my word to You?

Okay. Now list some of the things you have done in the past to sin against God:

1. _____
2. _____
3. _____
4. _____
5. _____
6. _____
7. _____
8. _____
9. _____
10. _____

Next to each thing you listed that you have done to God, I want you to write how God responded. Did He leave you?

Did He forgive you? Did He love you through it? Did He wait on you? Did He restore you? Did He deliver you?

If you are anything like me, you have lied to God. You have cheated on God. You have forsaken Him to please your flesh. You have turned your back on God, and you have not always kept your word or the vows you have made to Him. But He has not left me or you. He continues to love us, and He will never turn his back on us. He has delivered me and restored my marriage, and I believe that He will do the same for you and your marriage.

I hope you are still with me. If God can overcome all the hurt and pain that we inflict on Him, we can also overcome with His help. We can continue to love our spouse and move forward. It is God who has given us the strength to do so. So let's make a decision to leave the past in the past and move forward according to the word of God, having our minds set on pleasing God. If you really feel you need more time to process, then schedule individual therapy sessions with a Christian therapist and focus on you and God's will for you. But please don't get stuck here. Getting stuck in this place of feeling sorry for yourself because of what your spouse has put you through is detrimental to the health of the marriage, and beyond the marriage, it is detrimental to your physical, mental, and spiritual health. I have witnessed many of my clients get stuck saying things like, "But I want to know more about what he or she did before I can move on." My response is, "Okay, would you be okay with God pulling out your rap sheet of sin and reviewing it with you lie by lie, indiscretion by indiscretion?" Of course not. You don't want to revisit that. Why? Because you have repented and moved on, and so have you and your spouse. I don't mean to be insensitive, but this is where people become really sanctimonious and unable to stop pointing the finger at their spouse and move on. They convince themselves that they cannot forgive and move on. They decide that getting a divorce is in their best interest. They believe that things will be better in their life without the spouse. In some cases, this is true. In other cases, it is simply not true. It is your responsibility as a Christian to know the difference. I do not believe that the 40 to 50 percent of couples that get divorced get it right. Many people have prematurely made a decision to get a divorce instead of allowing God to heal and restore the marriage, and as a result, they are suffering from the loss of the marriage and a decision not to trust God.

Chapter 15
Just Trust Him

Iknow the decision to trust God with your marriage isn't as easy as words in a book make it sound. I, too, contemplated walking away from my marriage during a crossroad moment. The enemy almost had me convinced that walking away would be so much easier. That option was so tempting because the pain and the hurt and our inability to get on one accord was so intense that I wanted to react immediately. It was like holding my hand in fire that burned so intensely and being faced with the split-moment decision to pull my hand out of the fire and walk away. The problem is that many people walk away with an intense burn that will need to be tended to and nursed back to good health. Keeping my hand in the fire and allowing God to use the fire to refine the hand is also an option, but not a very comfortable one. God instructed me to keep my hand in the fire and allow Him to make it stronger. He used the fire, the thing that burned so badly, to also refine and heal our marriage. I decided to obey God and keep my hand in the fire. No matter how intense the flame got, I determined that I was committed to seeing it through to the end and believing God for a good outcome. Although the process was intense, God strengthened and refined me through it, and I came out on the other side of it healed and renewed, ready to move forward into a healthy marriage with a new way of seeing myself, my spouse, and God. Notice I said I. God instructed me to focus on the change that He was doing with me, the refining that was happening with me. I did not step out of what was going on with me to inquire about what God was doing with my husband during the time he was working with me. I kept my focus on God. I sought Him for what I needed as He exposed the areas in my life to which He wanted access. I trusted God with my husband. I was determined to be who God wanted me to be, and that alone left me with no time to focus on anything else but me and God. My favorite scripture during that crossroad moment was "Trust in the Lord with all your heart. Lean not to your own understanding. Acknowledge him in all of your ways, and he shall direct your path."

What I learned through our refining process is that "Love is patient, love is kind *and* is not jealous; love does not brag *and* is not arrogant, does not act unbecomingly; it does not seek its own, is not provoked, does not take into account a wrong *suffered*, does not rejoice in unrighteousness, but rejoices with the truth; bears all things, believes all things, hopes all things, endures all things" (I Corinthians 13:4-7, NASB). I came out on the other side of the crossroad softer, gentler, more tender, kinder, humbler, and readier to submit to God, deny my flesh, and serve my husband.

For the next 14 days, meditate on this scripture: "Trust in the Lord with all thine heart; and lean not unto thine own understanding. In all thy ways acknowledge him, and he shall direct thy paths. Be not wise in thine own eyes: fear the LORD, and depart from evil" - Proverbs 3:5-7, KJV.

Happily Ever After

Chapter 16
Let's Focus on Us

Marriage is a ministry ordained by God. In Genesis Chapter 2, "The Lord God caused a deep sleep to fall upon the man, and while he slept, took one of his ribs and closed up its place with flesh. And the rib that the LORD God had taken from the man he made into a woman, and brought her to the man"

Genesis 2:21-22, ESV.

Until this day, God continues to be responsible for presenting the woman to her husband. When a man finds a wife, he finds a good thing. I am convinced that when it is a real find, God is in it, showing the man his woman and giving him instruction on how he is to care for her, provide for her, and love her.

As Christians, we have the united responsibility of representing God in our oneness, being light in a dark world, making disciples by being an example that will lead the lost to confess Christ as Lord and Savior. Your marriage is to represent Christ and be displayed in a way that will encourage other couples to seek Christ for what He is displaying through the two of you. Your marriage should give couples hope that they can endure the hard times if they believe, obey, and apply the word of God as it relates to how they respect, love, and treat each other.

During one of our crossroads moments, I confided in my best friend, who at the time was a newlywed. She was discouraged by the fact that my husband and I were having problems that had us contemplating divorce as an option. After supporting me and encouraging me, she made a statement that penetrated my heart. She said, "If you guys can't make it, there is no hope for us." Her statement was confirmation that others are counting on us. They are looking to us to show them how this thing called marriage is done. God is counting on all of us to use our marriage to make disciples for him. As married couples, we are a billboard for Christ that says, "Yes we can." We can work through our differences, we can put God first, we can stay married, we can love each other the way that Christ loves us, and we can make disciples. Yes we can! My husband and I used the word of God to overcome our crossroad experience, and you can too.

1. If you were to divorce your spouse, list the people or families who will be impacted in a negative way.

_____

_____

_____

2. If you decide to get a divorce, what will you tell those people? How will you use your decision (to stay married or get a divorce) to minister to those people to whom you are closest?

_____

_____

_____

Chapter 17

What I Know for Sure Is...
That I Love Him
(My Testimony)

Love is constant and eternal. When everything around me is uncertain, the one thing I know for sure is that I love him and I want to spend the rest of my life on earth with him. I know that I want to honor God with my vows in this union. I want to push through the difficult times. I want to create new memories and reminisce about old ones. I want to build a legacy of fidelity, love, peace, harmony, and reconciliation that will stand like a pillar in our family for many generations to come.

I know for sure that I want forever. I want to hold him and be held by him. I want the late-night talks and the secret nods that only the two of us understand. I want the holding of hands when others are looking, and most importantly, when no one else is around. I want to feel like he wants to make my load in life lighter, protect me, and shield me from things to be concerned about.

I know for sure that I love him unconditionally, and I want to be loved by him without conditions. I want to be respected, protected, and honored. I want to respect, honor, and protect our union from the naysayers. I want agape love. I love him the way that God loves me, and I want his love for me to be an extension of the love that God has shown me. This is what I know for sure.

What Do You Know for Sure?

_____

_____

_____

When you approach a crossroad moment in your marriage, be intentional about meditating on what is loving, pure, and true about your union. Unfortunately, more often than not, what we do during a crossroad moment is meditate on what we do not want. "I don't want a spouse who will make me angry." "I don't want a spouse I cannot trust." "I don't want a spouse who does not support me." "I don't want a spouse who is lazy." And the list goes on and on. The scripture says focus on those things that are pure, loving, and true. Focus on your spiritual truth. Because we walk by faith and not by sight, spend some time speaking your spiritual truth into manifestation. Speak those things that be not as though they were. The word of God works. I am challenging you to try it by faith. Begin to speak the manifestation of God's word into your spouse's life and watch God begin to move. Your words are powerful in the ears of your mate. You have the ability to build your mate up with your words or tear your mate down with your words. Life and death are truly in the power of the tongue. Tell your spouse, "You are more than a conqueror. You can do all things through Christ who strengthens you. You are the righteousness of God. You are blessed and highly favored. You are healed. You are royalty." God will honor your faith in Him to transform your spouse and draw your spouse closer to Him.

Listen to God's whispers to you about who your mate is and how to best support your mate. Believe God. Know that God is a healer and a deliverer. Know that there is no circumstance too difficult for God to deliver the marriage from. Know that it is His will for the two of you to be together and honor the commitment that you both made before Him. Know that you will need to pick up your spiritual weapons and walk in the fruit of the spirit to be victorious on the other side of your crossroad experience.

Chapter 18

Understanding the Why

If I can convince couples to simply believe and apply I Corinthians 13:4-7 to their marriage, the divorce rate would immediately decrease by more than 50 percent. The world would look different if couples committed to staying together and being a light for Christ. Currently, when couples experience a crossroad moment, they have the worst disagreement they have ever had in life and they call the quits. How much different would things be if they extended patience and kindness to each other in the midst of the disagreement? How different would things be if they were very intentional about not becoming rude or arrogant during the disagreement? Would it make a difference if neither person was attached to getting his or her way? What if both people acknowledged the truth concerning the disagreement, humbled themselves, and allowed themselves to be vulnerable?

When I say focus on the truth, what I really mean is try to be mindful of what you are really arguing about. Many of us are deceived concerning what we are really arguing about. For example, a husband decided to run an errand for his mother instead of coming home in time for dinner with the family. On the surface, it may appear that the wife is upset about the husband not coming home first or making the family a priority over his mother. But underneath all of that, the real issue may be that the wife felt rejected, overlooked, unimportant, or insignificant, and all of these words are attached to real experiences and legitimate times when she was rejected or overlooked in her past. Her past experience has in turn triggered a plethora of emotions that she is now associating with her husband not being home for dinner on time. The argument is really about all the emotions she experienced when she felt this way in the past. If she is not careful, she will bombard her husband with all the emotions she is feeling when he enters the door, although these emotions have nothing to do with what he has actually done. The prudent thing to do is pull the husband aside when he returns home and say, "Honey, when you decided to run an errand for your mother instead of coming home for dinner on time, it triggered some old emotions from my past, and I felt overlooked, unimportant, and insignificant. I know when you decided to run an errand for your mom, it was not your intention to make me feel that way, but I want you to know that's how I felt. I was very angry at you, and I wanted to lash out at you until I realized that it was not your intent to make me feel that way because I know that is not who you are. You are not the type of person who would intentionally try to hurt me by running an errand for your mother. The Holy Spirit revealed to me that I was upset with you because I was reminded of when I had been rejected and overlooked in the past." The wife would be wise to follow up the conversation with her husband with a conversation with God in her prayer closet, asking him to heal those now exposed tender places that she has discovered are raw and unhealed.

Moving forward, before you react to your spouse's actions in a negative way, stop and pray. Ask God to reveal the truth to you about the emotions you are feeling. Ask Him to direct your response. This may sound foreign to you. You may feel like you must respond immediately, but you do not need to. If you are currently at a crossroad in your relationship, it is time to try something new. Doing what you have always done will not produce different results. When you stop to pray before responding in a way that is not pleasing to God, you actually give yourself some time to align your thoughts with the word of God and a moment to gain your composure and listen to the Holy Spirit. As Christians, we have the God-given task of learning how to discipline ourselves. The most difficult thing for me to submit to God was my tongue. I was raised by awesome parents who thought my freedom of speech was a God-given right. Their only stipulation was that I not disrespect them or my elders. For many years, I said whatever I wanted to say, only honoring those two stipulations. When I began to walk in close relationship with God, He had some serious work to do with this tongue of mine. Submitting my tongue to Him for his use was a journey in which I began to take pleasure. I wanted to be a better person. Although painful, I desired to have my flesh die, and I sought out opportunities to bridle my tongue. I wanted to move away from being quick to respond with harsh words to being gentle, loving, and kind. I asked God to teach me when to speak and when to simply be quiet. As I become closer to God, I want to be a doer of the word of God, not just a hearer of it. In James 1:19-20, James encourages Christians with these words: "Know this, my beloved brothers: let every person be quick to hear, slow to speak, slow to anger; for the anger of man does not produce the righteousness of God" (ESV). Your spouse is not your enemy. If you have been responding to your spouse like you are in battle, make a decision right now to change the way you speak to your spouse, your life partner, your best friend, your confidant, the bone of your bone, the flesh of your flesh. Ask God to help you identify what the source of the mean words is, and then ask Him to heal you in that deep place. You are a kind person, you are a loving person, you are a wonderful and supportive spouse. God created you to love your mate, to be kind to your mate, to support your mate, to pray for your mate, to comfort your mate, and stand side by side with your mate in difficult times. You have been called to impart wisdom to your spouse, not mean word. God has given you wisdom from above. James 3:17 says, "But the wisdom that is from above is first pure, then peaceable, gentle and easy to be intreated, full of mercy and good fruits, without partiality, and without hypocrisy" (KJV). The wisdom of God will cause you to be peaceable with your spouse and extend mercy and good fruits to your spouse. When we know this scripture and make a conscious decision to live this scripture, it is difficult to treat our spouse any other way than kind.

When God took off my blinders and allowed me to see how deep my words cut into the heart of my husband, I willingly gave over my sharp tongue to the Lord. I asked Him for a tongue that would give me the power to heal my husband in the deep places where I had cut him. God allowed me to walk in the wisdom of knowing that I had some work to do. As I was going through my crossroad experience, I became wise enough to understand that my husband's life and death was in the power of my words (my tongue). "Death and life *are* in the power of the tongue, And those who love it will eat its fruit" (Proverbs 18:21, NASB). God revealed to me how my husband often hung onto my words. In fact, my husband would often repeat things that I said to him as though they there were his own thoughts or words. God revealed to me that this happened because my words are important to my husband. It was revealed to me that he internalized my words. What I called him, he saw. Even when he rejected it externally, he had to wrestle with it internally because he saw us as one and he wanted to trust my words even when his spirit man said "no." I relinquished my sharp tongue to God because when I chose to speak things into my husband's life that were contrary to the word of God, it was revealed to me that I was destroying and tearing down the very fabric of his being.

Now I use my new tongue to build my husband up. As a wife, I had to give my sharp tongue over to God. Now I think first and speak last. I am intentional about navigating my marriage the way that God has called me to. I will walk away from a disagreement with my husband before I allow the enemy to use my tongue to paralyze my husband with hurtful words from my mouth, long after the argument has ended. Words hurt and words heal. When we say "I do" at the altar, we are committing to God and our mate to use our words to heal, love, and support one another.

We must remember at all times that our marriage is a ministry, and we are walking billboards for God at all times. We have been given the task of expressing his love for the church in our relationships. In order to do this, we must discipline ourselves to walk according to God's holy will. In 1 Corinthians 9:27, Paul said, "But I discipline my body and keep it under control, lest after preaching to others I myself should be disqualified" (ESV). Discipline yourself, your body, your mind, your soul, and your tongue so that you are available and useful to the body of Christ.

Be Patient & Heal

When we face adversity as couples, we often want to skip over the time to heal. Our desire is to get right back to the way we were before. But when God permits adversity to enter into our marriage, the intention is never to get us back to where we were before. The intent of adversity is to strengthen us, grow us, and move us further along to newer, greater heights and a better understanding of ourselves and God in our marriage. We should aim to grow through adversity. Each time my husband and I have embarked upon a crossroad moment in our marriage, we have come out on the other side of the experience stronger and with more clarity about our purpose and our responsibility to the kingdom of God. Most important of all, we both use that time individually to lean in closer to God.

Recently, I learned some interesting facts about the sequoia tree and how it responds in adversity. The sequoia tree is a tree that typically grows in a forest. This tree has the ability to grow 300 feet tall and over 200 feet wide in diameter. The sequoia tree can live 3,000 years or more. The adversities with which the sequoia tree is most familiar are high winds and forest fires. And although these trees grow in three feet of soil, high winds are not strong enough to destroy them because the roots are connected to other sequoia trees for strength and nourishing resources. A forest fire is known to destroy trees in its path for miles. Forest fires are not hot enough to destroy sequoia trees. Sequoia trees are fire resistant. In fact, forest fires are responsible for producing more sequoia trees. The heat from the fire causes the cones on the sequoia tree to pop and release seeds on the ground. When the seeds are released, they are fertilized by the ashes from the forest fire, and more sequoia trees grow. Adversity triggers growth among sequoia trees, and sequoia trees find their strength in being connected to one another.

Christian marriages have the ability to function like the sequoia trees. God made sequoia trees fire resistant. God also made Christian marriages divorce resistant. I know that the divorce rate is 40 to 50 percent, but that isn't because God did not give us the word that presents a full-proof plan to resist divorce. The plan that God has to keep the sequoia tree standing tall in the face of adversity is the same plan he has for us. Strong winds cannot knock the sequoia tree down regardless of how shallow its roots are because God has connected the roots of the sequoia trees to the roots of other nearby sequoia trees for strength. Christian couples don't have physical roots, but we have one another. When we connect as Christian couples, we strengthen and support one another so that we can continue to stand tall in the face of adversity.

Who is your accountability couple?

To whom has God connected you in the body of Christ for strength as it relates to your marriage?

If you do not have a couple in your life, ask God to send a couple and be patient. God may want you to just speak to Him for now.

....

Prayer:

God, please help me to use my tongue to lift, encourage, and speak life to my mate. Please prick my heart when I say things to my mate that are not pleasing in Your sight. Bless me to walk in wisdom as I deal with my mate. Keep it before me to show my mate the same love, kindness, gentleness, forgiveness, and respect that You show me. I declare that no weapon that is formed against this marriage will prosper and that every lying tongue will cease. Thank You for creating me in your image. And thank You for allowing me to look more and more like You with each passing day. Amen.

Meditate on this scripture:

"Can both fresh water and salt water flow from the same spring?"
(James 3:11, NIV).

Meditate on this scripture until God begins to speak to you concerning it.

Chapter 19
In Conclusion, Why Not You Two?

Lord, why us? My first response to the question I asked was, "Why not?" During one of our cross-road moments, I asked myself that question over and over again. I prayed, "Really, God? Lord, You can speak, and this experience will pass over us." I told God, "I don't have time for this. We are preachers, we teach marriage seminars, we counsel couples, we marry couples, we are good. No, this is not happening to us." I think what God really heard me say is we did not need to learn, grow, and mature in our union. Let me say this. Be careful not to challenge God! He allowed the process of refining us to begin. I learned that the question should have been, "Lord, what do You want us to learn from this experience so that we can use it to build Your kingdom?" No marriage is above the refining process. In fact, complacency does not benefit the union. Open your mind to the refining however it comes so that you can grow as an individual and your union will be strengthened. You will not learn how to fight lest you fight. Don't you recall that when you were in grade school, the kids who were the best fighters were those who fought. So fight. Fight for your marriage. Fight for the fire that used to once burn with passion between the two of you. Fight for your children. Fight for your legacy. Anyone can walk away, and anyone can check out or stay and be miserable. But those are not the only two options. Fight for the desire to embrace your mate like you once did. Fight for your heart to beat fast in his or her presence with excitement to be closer. Fight for the passion you felt on your wedding day. Fight for your eyes to light up again at the mere mention of your mate's name. Fight to consider your mate before your job, children, hobbies, and in-laws. Fight to look forward to seeing your mate at the end of a long day. Fight to feel what you felt the first time you kissed your mate. Fight for the refining process to be complete, making all things new. Fight to be strengthened so that you can strengthen your brothers and sisters.

Although my husband and I were not at each other's throat, we were still challenged with becoming complacent and dissatisfied with one another. We forgot what it felt like to desire each other's touch. Prior to the refining process, we had dismissed the importance of quality time together, affirming each other, caressing each other, flirting with each other, modeling a healthy relationship in front of our children, and surprising each other with special simple gifts just because. My experience and observation has taught me that persecution will come. Scripture says those who live godly shall suffer persecution (II Timothy 3:12). It is your spiritual response to the persecution that will determine whether or not the persecution will refine your union or destroy it.

Please allow me to warn you that the fight is not physical in nature.

> "[12] For we wrestle not against flesh and blood, but against principalities, against powers, against the rulers of the darkness of this world, against spiritual wickedness in high places.
>
> [13] Wherefore take unto you the whole armour of God, that ye may be able to withstand in the evil day, and having done all, to stand." (Ephesians 6:12-13, KJV)

Put on your whole armor of God so that as you fight for your marriage with spiritual weapons, the enemy's retaliation cannot penetrate you. Okay, now go to your closet and talk to God about you. Ask Him to help you look more like Him in the midst of this battle.

Focus on those things that are loving, pure, and true (Philippians 4:8). Allow me to remind you of some moments that may make the persecution worth fighting through. These are my experiences, but I am hoping you can relate to one or two of them:

The first time he held you like you were his

The first time he said, "I love you."

The day he asked you to spend forever with him

The birth of your first child

Having his hand to hold when the first contraction hit

Looking into his eyes at the altar and thinking that forever may not be long enough

The first kiss

The first intimate moment behind closed doors

The first time he made your eyes roll toward the back of your head

The first time he kissed you on the forehead (Oh, how I love that.)

....

Prayer:

God, I count it all joy that You are allowing us to be refined during this trial. Thank You for renewing our union. Thank You for helping me to take my focus off of me and put it on You and the ministry to which You have called us. Lord, help us to seek You first, as You add all things unto us. Amen.

Sources

Kimberly Bracewell-Thorpe, LMSW

About the Author

Kimberly Bracewell-Thorpe is a reverend from Pontiac, Michigan, living in Kalamazoo, Michigan. She is a licensed mental health clinician with a bachelor's degree in psychology from Oakland University and a master's degree in social work from the University of Michigan. Throughout her career, she has counseled several married and pre-married couples and has even had the pleasure of marrying many couples.

Kimberly and her husband are both entrepreneurs, and together they co-own three businesses: Let's Talk About It Community Mental Health Services, ACTS II Ministry For Teens, and Wet Paint and Palette. Her pride and joy is her family, as she is the mother of five children, Shalibria, Lauren, Kareem, Aniya, and Naomi, and the grandmother of four grandchildren, Alexa, Zaiden, Brielle, and Malani. In her free time, she enjoys traveling, spending time with her family and friends, and writing.

To learn more, visit her website at
KimberlyThorpeSpeaks.com

CREATING DISTINCTIVE BOOKS
WITH INTENTIONAL RESULTS

We're a collaborative group of creative masterminds
with a mission to produce high-quality books to position
you for monumental success in the marketplace.

Our professional team of writers, editors, designers,
and marketing strategists work closely together to ensure
that every detail of your book is a clear representation
of the message in your writing.

Want to know more?
Write to us at info@publishyourgift.com
or call (888) 949-6228

Discover great books, exclusive offers, and more at
www.PublishYourGift.com

Connect with us on social media

@publishyourgift

CPSIA information can be obtained
at www.ICGtesting.com
Printed in the USA
FFOW03n0628020518
46421811-48242FF